When my dad was on his heaven bed, I told him that there was a book inside of me—and that someday when I write it—I would dedicate it to him.

So, this is for you, Dad.

I love you!

"Danger: Don't read it if you want to remain the same! Finally, a startling book on evangelism that is about loving the lost rather than 'winning' them. This is a natural outflow of a revelation of Father's love. Well done Bob Johnson—you nailed it because you live it."

JOHN ARNOTT
CATCH THE FIRE
TORONTO, CANADA

"Bob Johnson has written a book that expresses the love of God in a pricelessly fresh, honest, and genuine way. He loves people enough to want them saved at any cost, but he also knows the only way to do that is to love them without an agenda for who they are. They need to encounter Jesus, and in the process experience a transcendent love they have never before known, or dreamed could exist. Religion is out; life is in. Love is aroused without pressure. Bob's stories are the fruit and evidence of freedom in our Perfect Savior. I am recommending this book to every hungry person I know who wants to evangelize!"

ROLLAND BAKER
DIRECTOR, IRIS MINISTRIES
PEMBA, MOZAMBIQUE

"Bob is a gifted evangelist and friend who has led many to the Lord through his passion to demonstrate the love of Jesus, even going to the darkest places to seek them out. His Love Stains will shift how we presently view evangelism and introduce a more natural way of loving people into the Kingdom. The way he shares his heart through his personal stories will stir us to 'leak' the love of Jesus to all whom we encounter. He understands that knowing the Father's love is one of the most important things we need to cultivate in our lives that will cause us stop for 'the one.' His passion is sure to inspire courageous love that reaches the deepest places of the heart."

HEIDI BAKER, PHD
FOUNDER, IRIS MINISTRIES
PEMBA, MOZAMBIQUE

"*Love Stains* shows you how a man on the streets openly displays the raw love of God. Bob has truly captured God's heart for evangelism. You will love the stories and the lessons learned within these pages. My bother in law IS the real deal! An excellent read."

BENI JOHNSON
BETHEL CHURCH SENIOR LEADER
AUTHOR OF *THE HAPPY INTERCESSOR*
REDDING, CALIFORNIA

"As I read this book I was deeply moved by the anointing that came off the pages. My life has been tremendously shaped and influenced by my Uncle Bob. In my younger years, he was largely responsible for instilling a heart to 'leak Jesus' everywhere I went. In this book he unloads story after story and reinforces them with the simplicity of the gospel. It's brilliant! I highly encourage you to read this book."

ERIC JOHNSON
BETHEL CHURCH SENIOR LEADER
AUTHOR OF *MOMENTUM: WHAT GOD STARTS NEVER ENDS*
REDDING, CALIFORNIA

"God has a desire that none would perish. His heart is burning for those who have never encountered His love to come face-to-face with His extravagant passion. The urgency of the hour requires the Church to be mobilized at another level. But we cannot do what we have always done.

In *Love Stains,* Bob Johnson tackles the challenge of approaching evangelism from a fresh perspective that will empower you to be confident walking it out. Every Christian I know has a heart to share Jesus with others, but that does not guarantee they will see fruit. Bob knows that can change. His message is not one of theory, but is born from years of seeing God touch the lives of those who have never been embraced by a loving Father. This book will change your life and in turn change the world around you."

BANNING LIEBSCHER
JESUS CULTURE DIRECTOR
REDDING, CALIFORNIA

"Before I moved to California, I remember hearing about Bob's ministry on the streets of San Francisco and desiring to see it for myself. Now I have had the privilege of witnessing roses given to prostitutes, meals given to the hungry, and love given to those the world calls 'unlovely.' Bob's ability to minister out of the Father's great love enabled him to present that love to the lost on the streets of San Francisco. This book is written out of a lifestyle, out of the experience of ministering to 'the very least of these my brethren.'

It is for this reason that I am honored to endorse a book written by a practitioner of the love of God. We don't need any more text books that are not the fruit of real lives. This book is the fruit of a life of ministry. The evangelist is not called to rattle off a gospel presentation and chalk up the number of converts, but to represent the extravagant love of our Heavenly Father, which results in transformed lives. This book will equip and encourage you, but I believe that it carries something more valuable: an impartation to live an authentic and courageous life that uncompromisingly presents the Good News of Jesus Christ through the practical and spoken expressions of our lives.

As Bob says, his goal in life is to give people a taste of Jesus; this book will give you a taste of *how*."

PAUL MANWARING
BETHEL CHURCH SENIOR LEADER
DIRECTOR OF GLOBAL LEGACY
AUTHOR OF *WHAT ON EARTH IS GLORY* AND *KISSES FROM A GOOD GOD*
REDDING, CALIFORNIA

"Bob Johnson is one of my treasured heroes. As a human being he is real, warmhearted, compassionate, and a genuine example of Christ's heart for mankind. As a modern-day evangelist, Bob is also a fearless risk-taker who has been willing to champion the cause of servant-based evangelism. And, as for Bob's book? What can I say except…awesome, awesome, awesome! I was greatly inspired by simply reading the outline of the manuscript. I quickly realized how effective this piece could be in the hands of a believer willing to trade 'casual religion' for a life of passionate love for humanity. This book is filled with real-life stories that capture the passion of a man's heart to fulfill the Great Commission of Christ."

LARRY RANDOLPH
FOUNDER AND PRESIDENT OF LRM

"If you've never met Bob then it's like you've never seen the moon. Yes, you'll have to look up to see either, but like the moon, Bob shines the brightest at night. Trained in the 'Tenderloin' of San Francisco, California, Bob is a redemption-seeking missile. Any and all who find themselves at the end of Hope's rope are likely to look up and see Bob lowering himself down into the hole to bring them Spirit-led encouragement. Bob's passion and courage will inspire you to see the lost through the eyes of a loving and powerful Father."

DANNY SILK
BETHEL CHURCH SENIOR LEADER
AUTHOR OF CULTURE OF HONOR, LOVING YOUR KIDS ON PURPOSE, AND POWERFUL AND FREE.
REDDING, CALIFORNIA

"I've known Bob Johnson for two decades and I've always been challenged by his raw, unique, yet effective means of winning the 'tough' cases. Bob is the real deal in a time where many evangelists are afraid to win souls outside of the pulpit. Bob's new book, Love Stains is a fresh, inspiring, equipping and prophetic manual of how to see an awakening on the streets and in the marketplace. Too many believers lock up with fear when they witness. As Children of the King we shouldn't experience panic on the streets...we should cause it! This book will make you a Dread Champion against modern day darkness and a compassionate awakener amongst the current lost generation. This is a must read that you will not put down!"

SEAN SMITH
DIRECTOR OF SEAN SMITH MINISTRIES/POINTBLANK INTL.
AUTHOR OF I AM YOUR SIGN & PROPHETIC EVANGELISM
TWITTER: @REVSEANSMITH

"There is so much crazy stuff done in the name of God that it makes me want to become a secret follower of Jesus. In the twenty-first century church, it is often hard to distinguish between evangelism and aggressive marketing. The goal of evangelism has been reduced to getting someone to pray a prayer, raise his or her hand, or come forward. I have no problem with anything a person does to take a step of faith to receive Jesus Christ and become a new creation. But if someone can be talked into converting to Christianity, they can be talked out of it. True Christianity must be experienced, not intellectualized. It's with the heart, (not the head) that people believe and are transferred out of the kingdom of darkness and thrust into the Kingdom of His beloved son.

Love Stains is a radical departure from manipulative evangelism. Bob Johnson takes us on a profound journey: Like a servant sent out to look for a bride for his wealthy master, Bob pursues heaven's treasures among earth's trash. *Love Stains* reads like a supernatural romance and adventure novel. It's a powerful story of Believers who reach into the darkest places of the planet to touch the broken, the rejected, and the poor with the irresistible love of Jesus. This book is a must read for every Christian who is hungry to make a difference in the lives of the lost."

Kris Vallotton
Senior Associate Leader, Bethel Church
Co-Founder of Bethel School of Supernatural Ministry
Author of nine books including
The Supernatural Ways of Royalty and *Spirit Wars*
Redding, California

"I first met Bob and Kimberly Johnson when they were speaking at Heidi and Rolland Baker's Harvest School in 2008. I was blown away by the amazing stories in reaching out to the *least*, *lost*, and *last* that Bob told. I had never heard such courage, such creativity, or such passion in reaching out with the love of Jesus. Since then Bob and Kimberly have ministered here in Scotland, and they have stirred up a courageous faith within this nation again. They have the ability to 'do the stuff,' but also to draw up others into this extraordinary ministry. I am sure that *Love Stains* will challenge, incite, and provoke—that is what is on Bob's heart—the Church to awaken to reaching the lost with new passion. Along with this, it will also encourage, excite, and motivate a whole generation who have been waiting to hear a new call to give their lives for the precious ones that Jesus gave his life for."

ALAN MCWILLIAM
CHURCH LEADER, WHITEINCH CHURCH OF SCOTLAND, GLASGOW
CHAIRMAN, CLAN (NEW WINE SCOTLAND)

"I've known Bob Johnson for a long time and his heart has always burned for seeing people won to Christ. Seems like in our modern culture everyone wants to have the 'big crusades' and nobody wants to do the one on one. As Bob says in his book, "Everyone wants to know that God knows their name." Does that diminish the effectiveness of a big crusade, absolutely not. But there is no substitute for personal evangelism. It's not complicated, it doesn't take some mystical formula to reach people, you just meet them where they are. People want to hear from YOU, they want to know what God has done for YOU, they want to know that Christ has made a difference in YOU. They want to know God is real.

There's great information in this book but if you don't make a conscious decision to put it into practice, then it's just words on a page. Make it personal. "You are a walking encounter with Jesus."

PASTOR BILL WILSON
FOUNDER AND SENIOR PASTOR
METRO MINISTRIES

Contents

Published by:

THERE IS NO BOX

Unless otherwise marked, scripture quotations are from the New King James
Version. Copyright © 1982 by Thomas Nelson, Inc. Used by permission.
All rights reserved.

Scripture quotations marked MSG are taken from The Message. Copyright ©
1993, 1994, 1995, 1996, 2000, 2001, 2002. Used by permission of NavPress
Publishing Group.

Cover Artist, Matthew Anderson, aka "Ginozko."
ginozko.com Facebook.com/ginozko

Interior Designer, Randy Womack

ISBN-10: 0988499215

ISBN-13: 978-0-9884992-1-8

Printed in U.S.A.

Distributed by:

red arrow

Red Arrow Media
Redding, California

ACKNOWLEDGEMENTS

Mom, thank you for always believing! You taught me what could be, not what couldn't happen, and for that I will be forever grateful. You also showed me the power of a mother's love—I love you!

To the Red Arrow Media publishing team, wow, you are all amazing! You're professionalism coupled with friendship is just what I needed to accomplish this project. A special thanks to Vanessa and Jess for your tireless hours of work and seeing this reach its potential. And I cannot forget to thank my friend Randy Womack. Your friendship and love to me is astounding. Plus the many hours you spent on this project—thank you my friend.

To my brother Bill Johnson and my other brother Mario Murillo. I wouldn't be here right now writing this if it wasn't for what the two of you have poured into my life. I am forever indebted to you both—thank you for loving me so well!

To my wife Kimberly, my favorite on this earth. Life with you is what Heaven is all about. Thank you for saying yes on that wonderful day and everyday since. I "lover" you forever!

FOREWORD BY BILL JOHNSON

Love Stains is a profound book that was thirty years in the making. For eleven of those years, it was my privilege to have Bob work with me as an associate pastor. His primary responsibility was youth. Bob is my brother, ten years my junior.

The impact of his life is beyond measure. A very high percentage of the leaders from his youth group are pastors and missionaries today. They serve all around the world. The heart for nations, the heart for souls, became a permanent fixture in that generation. I know this firsthand. My three children were a part of his team. And the effect of this evangelist's life has left a permanent mark on theirs.

The evangelist's burning heart is contagious, as they have discovered something that brings exceedingly great joy to the Father. Papa God desires the restoration of every person through encountering his love. It is normal to leave the presence of a true evangelist with a burden for the lost. It shouldn't be any other way. Bob is no exception. He burns for the lost in a way that few have experienced, and he unconsciously imparts that passion to those around him.

What is unique about Bob—and therefore this book—is his complete lack of religious pressure to evangelize. He has correctly brought this great subject back to its foundation: "for God so loved the world…" When love is the source and motivation for evangelism, people cease being projects to ease our conscience and become vessels into whom our Father desires to pour the fullness of His blessings. Showing God's love is the great privilege in life.

But what is especially unique about Bob is the target of his ministry. He sincerely prioritizes those who cannot pay him back in any way. In other words, his focus is on the most broken and despised people on the earth. He has the most unusual gift of calling greatness out of these broken people. I've watched him as an army of people form around him that would do anything for him, even take a bullet. These folks have already been to hell and back and have a refreshingly simple standard: love God with all their hearts, and love people at any cost. I've been moved by this army of "heaven's treasures."

Without question, salvation remains the greatest miracle of all. That obviously means to receive the forgiveness of sins and be brought into the family of God. But salvation is more. It also means healing and deliverance. I cannot tell you how happy I am to see this evangelist present a gospel that will not only get people to Heaven, but also give them a taste of Heaven while here on earth through the freedom God provided for all who call upon His name. Bob operates in great power. And people really get free. Totally free.

Several times my eyes welled up with tears while reading this book. I am wonderfully broken inside as I recall story after story of amazing grace displayed through this man…a man I am honored to call my brother.

Let the reader beware: You are about to be ignited by a presentation of evangelism that everyone can and must do. Your heart will burn with hope that you can be used almost effortlessly in a gift most thought was inaccessible. This book is practical and powerful. It is simple yet profound. It presents our assignment in a way that will challenge your thinking, but will also provide a pathway to follow that is actually doable. Enjoy this great adventure!

BILL JOHNSON
BETHEL CHURCH SENIOR LEADER
AUTHOR OF *WHEN HEAVEN INVADES EARTH* AND *HOSTING HIS PRESENCE*
REDDING, CALIFORNIA

Foreword By Mario Murillo

In 1999 we took on a project that was impossible. We rented the famous Cow Palace in San Francisco for seven days. We had to try and fill 16,000 seats seven times. Plus we had to do this in what is known as the most notoriously anti-God city in America.

Unless we hit the streets, there would be no hope of getting the job done. We needed a man to handle the streets of San Francisco. Bob Johnson was that man. What he and his team did for six months on those desperate streets is an additional chapter in the book of Acts.

They mounted an invasion that is unequalled in the 300-year history of San Francisco. Miracles of healing happened among the thousands of homeless living under freeways. Prostitutes, addicts, children in the sex trade, and all of the other victims that the city hides beneath her beauty got a direct dose of the love of Jesus and the power of the Holy Spirit.

What was just as remarkable was the balance that Bob struck between the timeless power of the Holy Spirit and "new inventions." God gave Bob miracles and great ideas.

We are drowning in books. All too often, they are nothing but theories. This book is the culmination of all that Bob has received from Jesus and tested in the crucible of street ministry. It is controversial, and it should be. We are wasting precious time on the sacred cows of church tradition. We are losing ground fast and need act with violent faith to turn things around.

God is ready to do the greatest things He has ever done to win lost souls and destroy the works of Satan. This book will help get God's best and break the fear and doubt that holds you back.

Mario Murillo
Founder of Mario Murillo Ministries
Author of *Critical Mass* and
I Am the Christian the Devil Warned You About

INTRODUCTION

Do you feel uneasy when you hear the word *evangelism*?

Does it conjure up painful images of going door to door with tracts and a foreboding sense of obligation and guilt?

If it does, you are not alone. Sharing the good news—for most—has become complicated; a painful chore that leaves many of us feeling uncomfortable, awkward, and even ashamed.

The other side of the coin shows Billy Graham. While Christians around the planet admire him, they also know that the odds of personally leading a crusade anytime soon are definitely not in their favor.

The purpose of this book is to show you a different picture of evangelism altogether.

That's right. No tracts. No door to door. No cookie-cutter image of what an evangelist should look like.

It's time to shift every preconceived idea you have about evangelism.

Imagine God using you just the way you are to touch the people in your everyday life. A simple smile, a gentle word of encouragement, a prophetic statement, a gift given in due season, the courage to hold the heartbroken, the ability to love the unlovable, healing the sick, and delivering the oppressed—all because of Jesus in you—just by you being you.

Imagine being Jesus in the grocery store.

Imagine being Jesus in your office.

Imagine being Jesus to your family.

Imagine being Jesus to the world.

What would happen?

Well…to find out, you'll need to keep reading.

WHY ARE YOU READING THIS BOOK?

Let me guess. Your desire is to be more like Jesus.

Maybe you are someone who has taken a few evangelism classes—that never paid off.

Maybe you're someone who is fed-up with evangelism. You're tired of the guilt trips and pressure, and you feel like giving up on sharing your faith.

Maybe you are tired of feeling like you are giving a sales-pitch for a product few are buying.

Or maybe you've heard the stories—the testimonies of miraculous events happening around the world—and you want some stories of your own.

Whoever you are and whatever your reason for reading this book, I believe that God has placed it in your hands for a specific purpose.

In these pages, my desire is to show you a picture of Father's heart. I want you to know that evangelism is not about closing a sale.

Evangelism is about loving people.

If you are filled with Jesus, you cannot help but "leak" Him everywhere you go. This is something every believer should do naturally. It is as easy as breathing, as beautiful as the restoration of family, and as fulfilling as a dream come true. Nothing gives Father more joy than watching you *be* Jesus with skin on to a hurting world.

You don't need another manual or five-step plan for leading people to Father.

All you have to do is start loving people.

It really is that simple.

What Is an Evangelist?

The basic definition of an evangelist is "one who brings good news." Pretty uncomplicated. Which is how I like to keep it.

As you have probably guessed, I am an evangelist, but I've not written this book for evangelists. I wrote it for the rest of the Church because, believe it or not, the number one job of an evangelist is to equip the Church to do the work of ministry (Eph. 4:11-12).

Look it up. That's right, my primary job is to equip you to minister and share the gospel (which is my secondary job).

I can safely assume that all of us want to be carriers of the good news. The chapters of this book are filled with keys on how to do just that—and to free you from all the religious junk that has kept you from doing that in the first place.

Now, I want to cover some ground rules before you dive in.

GROUND RULES

Many times throughout this book, I will be referring either directly or indirectly to the rule, not the exception to the rule.

As you read, there will probably be times an exception to something that I've said will pop up in your mind like a blinking light. Don't get sidetracked by the flashy exceptions. Continue to read and allow the Holy Spirit to work.

Let's face it: Most rules have exceptions. God sometimes mixes things up for us. He doesn't always work in the same way. He's creative.

As you read, ask the Holy Spirit to teach you. Ask Him to open your eyes to see new things and your ears to hear new revelation. This book is by no means the end-all book on evangelism; it is merely the beginning.

FINAL THOUGHTS BEFORE TAKING THE PLUNGE

So you've made it to the end of the introduction. I want to pray for you before you go any farther. Here goes: May the following words ignite a fire inside of you so that you would see yourself—everywhere you go—as a carrier of good news. May you leak Jesus onto everyone and everything. May you feel His love pouring out of you like never before. May you be freed from any and all performance and pressure agendas. And that as a result, His life inside of you will bring life.

Good reading! And happy Jesus-leaking!

Love,

Bob Johnson

one

FREE FOOT-WASHING, SIR?

It's a story about socks, some messed up feet, a cool van, and Jesus.

And it's one I love to tell—primarily because I love telling stories about when Jesus shows up.

My name is Bob Johnson. You'll learn more about me as you keep reading, but for now, all you need to know is that I love Jesus, I love my family, and I love the streets.

It's a pleasure to meet you.

Okay, back to my story. Listen up now. It's an important one, and it begins under Highway 101 in a homeless camp in San Francisco one, cold night.

It was the usual with my team ministering on the streets: We had our Cosmo Van, and we were handing out socks. Our Cosmo Van was a box van we converted into a cosmetology shop on wheels. We could drive it anywhere and give prostitutes and homeless people a haircut or wash. You would be surprised how many little luxuries—like haircuts—most of us take for granted.

Like I said, we were also handing out socks to our friends, who frequently would walk miles each day for a single hot meal. Why? Because on the often cold and wet streets of San Francisco, to a homeless person, socks are the equivalent of gold.

People who live on the streets wear socks until they are literally falling apart, and often doing more harm then good. Each day is a fight to survive, and needless to say, feet are not a priority. Rotting skin and fetid foot sores are a common and painful reality.

I passed out socks for a while, watching as many of the homeless would remove their weathered boots and peel off their socks in pieces. They would then slowly slide on their new, clean, white socks, undoubtedly wiggle their toes, and give a faint grin of gratitude.

Taking a minute to breathe, I watched people go into the Cosmo Van looking one way—*weathered* would be a good term—and coming out looking…well, they looked wholly different. They came out looking loved.

Accepted

Like someone cared.

They didn't look discarded anymore. One miracle after another came out of the van, and I couldn't help but express to God how awesome I thought it was.

"Yes. It is wonderful, Bob." He answered.

Then He began to explain why these transformations were taking place. It was because we were using the most powerful gift He had given us.

Love

Now as great as it was that night to see people transformed by the love happening in the Cosmo Van, I wanted to find ways of using the gift of love that went beyond haircuts. So, I started to brainstorm with Holy Spirit.

My thoughts turned away from the van, and I looked back at the team handing out socks. My eyes locked on foot after terribly dilapidated foot, and my heart suddenly cried out, "God, help me to go beyond just meeting a need with socks. Help me to take it to another level of blessing. I want Your love to be shown through me." I waited a minute. And then the idea hit me, "We could wash their feet!"

It seemed to come out of nowhere—but it stuck. Furthermore, I immediately felt God's heartbeat on this cry from the depths of my soul to bless my homeless friends' feet and to love the unlovely. And together, with my team, we turned this idea into a reality.

By our next street outreach, Ben Armstrong, an invaluable member of our team, had set up foot washing stations along the side of the Cosmo Van.

FOOT WASHERS, INC.

I figured that, since this was my idea, I should do the honors and perform the first footbath. Scanning the homeless camp, I spotted the most needy looking person in my line of sight.

I approached him, "Sir, may I wash your feet?" I asked with as much tenderness as I could muster, despite maybe a bit too much excitement. Obviously, I'm not big on small talk.

He looked at me like I was from another planet and emphatically said, "No," as he walked away.

"It would be an honor for me if you would allow me to wash your feet," I called after him.

"No thanks."

I knew this idea was from God, and I wasn't about to let that man get away. It was time for bribery.

"Do you need fresh socks?"

I already knew the answer. Of course he needed socks.

He stopped, turned around, and answered quietly, "Yes."

"If you let me wash your feet, I will give you TWO pairs of socks."

He thought for a moment and then said timidly, "Okay."

I walked with him over to the chair we had prepared and asked him to sit down. I carefully removed his shoes, not at all prepared for what I was about to see.

Open sores covered both feet. An intense rash covered his calves and ankles, and the smell was somewhat overwhelming. It was as though he had not taken his shoes off in years, much less had his feet washed.

My heart welled up with compassion. What had this poor man lived through? Where had these feet been? Lowering his feet into the warm water, I carefully began to wash his feet.

And then, in a moment, there He was.

Father had come to watch. I felt His presence everywhere. It was thick and tangible—and I no longer smelled the stench that had filled the air just moments before. Instead, a heavenly sweet aroma surrounded me. It was almost an out of body experience.

As my hands rubbed Neosporin into his festering sores, Father gave me a prophetic word to speak over him. The result of this encounter was that the man who wanted nothing more than a pair of socks got something much better. He got Jesus. Right then and there, with new socks on his feet and the smell of heaven penetrating the cold night air, he gave his heart to the Savior. He became a brand new man.

The truth is, when we touch people, the power of Heaven is released and things happen. Love is powerful. We carry an astounding anointing, just as Isaiah prophesied:

And it shall come to pass in that day, that his burden shall be taken away from off thy shoulder and his yoke from off thy neck, and the yoke shall be destroyed because of the anointing (Isa. 10:27).

When we love people by washing their hair or feet, or by giving them a manicure, our faith moves Heaven, and the anointing flows, removing yokes and lifting burdens. Through our hands, the love of Father within us literally covers a multitude of sins, allowing people to receive a touch from Jesus and be forever changed (1 Pet. 4:8). That's why people were coming to the Cosmo Van or the foot wash station one way and coming out completely new.

Door to Door

You know, Jesus said, *"...Inasmuch as you have done it to one of the least of these my brethren, you did it to Me"* (Matt. 25:40).

Think about that.

According to this verse, I was *literally* washing the feet of Jesus when I washed that homeless man's feet. That's why Father came down to see what I was doing. He wanted to watch His Son get His feet washed.

By washing that homeless man's feet, I was simply obeying the command Jesus gave to His disciples in John 13, when Jesus told Peter that if He didn't wash His feet, Peter couldn't have any part of Him. Then Jesus told His twelve friends to follow His example and serve one another by following suit and washing each other's feet.

Such a simple act, if done out of obedience to Father, can bring such freedom, restoration, hope, and life. That night, for that man, it brought salvation. And two new pairs of socks...

It is profound what happens when you simply wash someone's feet.

But, to be completely honest, I didn't start off as a foot washer— though I wish I had.

Like most evangelists, I started out as a salesman of sorts. You could say I started out door to door.

Picture the following:

It's a bright sunny day in a nice suburban neighborhood. I approach a house and politely knock on the front door.

The door opens, I take a breath, brace myself, and begin, "Hi, my name is Bob Johnson. How are you today?"

I'm relieved. It's a nice-looking motherly woman. She leaves the door open and cheerfully says, "I'm fine. How can I help you?"

Giving her my brightest smile, I answer, "I was in your neighborhood today, and I wanted to make sure that the condition of your heart is ready to meet God someday." I'm feeling confident. No matter what her response will be, I know what to say. Because of my training and years of experience, I am ready for anything. I've got this down.

"I'm sorry, but I don't believe in God," the lady responds.

"What do you mean you don't believe in God?" I ask, expressing as much shock as I can muster. "I'm from the First Church of Heaven on the corner of Right Street and Wrong Avenue, and I'm compelled to tell you that, because of your last statement, you will be joining Satan in Hell."

At this, her eyebrows begin to arch in annoyance. But I ignore her response and barrel forward in an attempt to finish my memorized speech before she slams the door in my face.

"Please understand that Hell wasn't made for you, but because of your stupidity, you're going to go there. The fire will burn you, but will not consume you; the worms will gnaw on your flesh, but it will not be devoured. You are very fortunate that I showed up today, because I can show you the way."

This woman is exceptionally patient and good-natured and so the door miraculously stays open. I continue, "Ma'am, if you pray this prayer with me and really believe what you are praying, there is still hope for you. Will you pray with me now?"

Despite giving her my most hopeful and compassionate look, she is done listening. "I am not interested!" She states and shuts the door firmly, while I walk proudly on to her next-door neighbor's, never giving her a second thought or prayer.

Okay. Stop picturing.

Admittedly, that is an extreme scenario and don't worry—I never told a sweet woman she was stupid and going to hell.

Don't get me wrong; I am not against going door-to-door to share Jesus. I've done it, several times. Many people meet Jesus this way.

But it does highlight why evangelism is painful for a lot of people.

Nobody wants to be that guy.

That guy is scary. The whole process is scary.

WHY DO WE DO THAT

Why does evangelism sometimes feel like selling vacuums door-to-door?

Here is why: Many of us have been trained to use a bag of tools and methods to share the gospel. More often than not, those methods become the focus instead of Jesus. When that happens, we can end up selling and manipulating instead of serving and sharing Father's gift of salvation and love.

And beyond being weighed down by a bunch of speeches and tracts, the fact remains that many Christians secretly fear sharing their faith—and feel guilty about it. When you "fail" to share Jesus with those you meet on the subway, with other parents at your children's sporting events, and with your neighbors and co-workers, you will—if you are like most Christians—beat yourself up about it. Sharing Jesus is the Great Commission. If you fail in that, it's like failing being a Christian.

I hate that ashamed "I've failed God, *again*..." feeling.

And in my past, I've felt it a lot.

When I first started to evangelize and work on developing my gift, if I didn't share Jesus with every person I came in contact with, I condemned myself for being an irresponsible believer. And worse, I would chastise others from the pulpit for doing the same, "Real Christians save the lost!"

I want to take a moment to apologize on behalf of evangelists everywhere—including myself—who have preached those sermons. Believe me, the hearts of most evangelists are good.

We want people to experience the love of Father.

But our zeal has often taught and modeled methods that border on, and occasionally use, manipulation and fear. That hasn't been our intent, but our love for the lost has often compelled to us to "do whatever it takes" to awaken the Church and to save the world—even at the expense of the Body. And we need your forgiveness.

BATHTUB PRAYER

When I was a young man, a traveling minister came to my brother Bill's church in Weaverville to teach about prayer. I don't remember the name of the guest, but I vividly remember the outcome of his visit. While he didn't preach in a condemning way, by the time he was done, I felt like the most worthless Christian ever born. This preacher testified about how he would get up at 4 a.m. each morning to meet with God.

What? 4 a.m.

Is that what it took to be a good Christian? If that was the case, I guessed I would have to start waking up at 4 a.m. too. So that night, I set my alarm and prepared for an awesome morning.

When 4 a.m. came, I prayed like there was no tomorrow. I prayed with fervency for every person I knew.

Then I looked at the clock. I had been praying for all of ten minutes. This was going to be harder than I thought. I felt a nudge from the Spirit of God to lay prostrate before Him, so I did. And the next thing I knew, it was 8 a.m.

Waking up to that realization was awful. I had failed God again.

The next morning, I was more determined to succeed than ever. Again, I set my alarm for 4 a.m., and as soon as it buzzed, I jumped out of bed and began to pray. I prayed for everything and everyone I could think of. I prayed for every country that was on my heart. I prayed for the future. I prayed for my city. I prayed for the poor. When I had finished, I looked at the clock. It was 4:15 a.m.

Another 45 minutes to go.

Five more minutes passed before I felt led to kneel before God. I woke up at 7:45 a.m.—still kneeling. My legs had fallen asleep, and I couldn't stand up.

By this time you can imagine my frustration with myself.

The next morning, I decided to take drastic measures to insure my success. I woke up at 4 a.m. and headed straight for the bathtub. I figured that if I stood in the tub and happened to fall asleep, I would fall. If I fell, I would get hurt, and if I got hurt, I would deserve it because I could not tarry with God. As you can imagine, this didn't end well.

All of that goes to say that my venture into early morning prayer wasn't exactly, shall we say, successful.

So, what was my problem?

It was this: I tried to imitate the preacher, to create out of his life a method or tool I could apply to my own. In doing that, I forgot to ask Father what He wanted me to do to deepen our relationship.

God obviously wanted this minister up that early.

He had something else planned for me.

We all do this more than we care to admit. In fact, this sort of copycatting is how most of the Church trains people to evangelize. And the result is that we have ended up with Christians who do not want to share Jesus because it makes them feel like salespeople, actors, or just tongue-tied.

TOOLS OF THE TRADE

Good salespeople require tools to help them sell. They refine their sales pitches and perfect their power points and demonstrations.

Evangelism is sadly often treated the same way. There are pitches, power points, and demonstrations galore. It is relatively easy to master many of the tools used to share Jesus—but in the process—lose our connection with Jesus' heart.

Who wants to be a salesperson for Jesus? Did Jesus ever ask you to be His salesman? I mean, besides the fact that most people are majorly turned off by salesmen—no offense intended if that happens to be your line of work—the fact remains that Jesus asked you to be…Jesus.

He asked you to be Him.

That's a big difference.

Jesus didn't manipulate people with tools and methods. He listened to the Holy Spirit and did what Father was doing (John 5:19).

That's it.

He never ministered to two people the same way.

He was always doing something slightly shocking, always effective, and completely connected to Father, like putting mud on a blind man's eyes or talking with a prostitute.

The simplicity of His presence in people's homes caused the very dynamic of their lives to change (John 9:1-12; Luke 19:1-10).

Listening to the Holy Spirit like this is risky. But in reality, listening is not the scary part—trusting Him enough to obey is.

I'm not saying that tools are necessarily bad. God has given us many tools, methods, or ways of doing things, and they have their place. Proverbs 21:31 says, *"The horse is prepared for the day of battle, but victory belongs to the LORD."*

The point is, do what God says.

If He says to use a certain tool or method, use it. But if He says to do something else, don't revert back to your comfort zone or to how you have been trained.

Tracts aren't bad. Neither is prayer, prophecy, healing, Bible knowledge, or any other number of tools. These are all wonderful gifts from God—when used correctly—but they are not formulas for evangelism. Only God knows the key that will unlock the sinner's heart. And only God can tell you what that key is—no method or gift or amount of knowledge can do that.

Once He reveals what that key is, you can use it to give an encounter with Jesus that will lead them into the Kingdom.

NAMES

Remember when Pre-Owned Cars were called Used Cars, Custodial Engineers were called janitors, and bath tissue was called toilet paper?

Guess what? Changing the name doesn't change the product.

The same is true of evangelism.

It's not about making our approach more user-friendly or seeker-sensitive. It's the truth that sets people free, not the car the truth is delivered in. So if our attention is on the car—and not the truth, Jesus—the end result of our evangelizing will be void.

And if we are not careful, the way we deliver Jesus becomes our priority rather than the people who actually need Him. Believe you me—that is not God's heart. He loves the lost.

He left ninety-nine to go after one (Luke 15:3-5).

He is looking for those who will get into the middle of His heart for the lost—those who will cry and grieve and understand the value of every single human being.

In evangelism, our motivation must be rooted in the revelation that God bankrupted Heaven to give His only Son in order to save one.

Just one.

GUILTY!

During my "mastery of the methods phase," on several occasions, I found myself using the methods to convict people of their sins and then showing them the way out. I became a skilled surgeon, able to use the "knife of conviction" to cut deep.

The problem was that if people could be persuaded into the Kingdom with human tools, usually they could be persuaded out of the Kingdom just as easily. I know that through God's grace, *"All things… work together for good to those who love God"* (Rom. 8:28)—even seeds that were planted and harvested before their time. Nevertheless, I don't look back on that season with pride.

It's not my job to convict anyone.

It's the Holy Spirit's (John 16:8).

Once I met a young man who told me, "I can't receive Jesus because I can't stop smoking pot."

I told him, "I didn't tell you to stop smoking pot."

"You didn't?" he asked, explaining to me that other Christians had told him as much.

I responded, "I didn't say you need to quit smoking pot. All I'm saying is that you need to come to Jesus."

The Church has tried to create a one size fits all formula for making disciples, but God has some different ideas about making sons and daughters. We should not excuse sin, but we must remember that Paul said sin for one guy is not necessarily sin for his next-door neighbor (Rom. 14). Even in matters that are obviously sin, the result of trying to put our personal convictions on other people will never bring them into true freedom.

Only Holy Spirit's conviction has the power to set people free. When we convict, we tie people up with rules and regulations they can't live up to. And that's definitely not the gospel.

Many of our convictions are true. What's difficult for us to understand is that our convictions may not be the living truth for the moment.

The Holy Spirit does not convict any of us of *all* of the areas of sin or weakness in our lives at once. Yet so often this is what we want to do to unbelievers or new believers. Instead, we must lead people to truth by showing them God's Word and God's heart. Rather than teaching what's right and wrong, we should share how to hear God's voice.

When people learn to listen to Father, they will discover for themselves what's wrong and receive the power to change their behavior. When they hear from the Big Man Himself, it's a done deal.

ARE YOU SELLING SOMETHING?

The next time you are talking to someone about Jesus, ask yourself, "Am I thinking about my next line or move, or am I actually listening and concerned for the person I'm talking with?"

People are smart. They can sense if you have an agenda or whether you are genuinely concerned about them.

One night on Market Street in San Francisco, I approached a man and asked him if he needed prayer. That's a pretty straightforward question. I use it a lot on the streets. But even asking if someone needs prayer can be a formula.

This particular night, I was acting out of a formula, and I failed to see that this man wasn't interested in prayer because he was freezing. When I offered prayer, the man's response was, "No. I'm cold, and I have no place to sleep for the night."

Duh! I thought to myself. My team and I quickly gave him some blankets and then helped him build a cardboard shelter for the night.

When we were finished, he said, "Now I'll take that prayer."

If I had been a little more concerned for the homeless man on the cold San Francisco streets, I would not have jumped so quickly to the prayer question. I am eager to pray with people because I have seen them, time and time again, experience a touch from Heaven. However, the reality is that prayer is not always the most immediate need.

Sometimes you just need to feed someone.

Or hug someone. Or help someone get warm.

We have been taught that the bottom line is, "If I can get 'John

Q. Sinner' to pray the sinner's prayer with me, everything will be okay." That means our goal is the measure of success—praying "the sinner's prayer" with someone—rather than giving someone a Heaven encounter. But just one encounter with Jesus will do more in a person's life than an eternity of Roman's Road Illustrations, which have little effect on non-believers with no Bible knowledge anyway.

Only as we listen to His voice will we ever be able to truly touch people's hearts with Father's love and the power of salvation.

And as long as we are on the subject, I want you to know that there is no rush. We do not need to seal the deal "right now, or else."

God is not in a hurry.

He loves people too much to leave their destinies in your hands. God's love and grace are breathtaking and beyond comprehension. He will set up as many roadblocks in the lives of those who are on Hell's Highway as He wants to.

We are blessed just to be one of those divine appointments.

THE BBQ

Don't worry if your head is spinning by now. I just hit pretty hard and fast on some things that have been programmed into a lot of us. But the truth is, sometimes old mindsets need to be chucked out or thrown into the fire.

There is only one place for religious cows, and that is the BBQ.

Never heard of a religious cow? No problem. I'll explain: A religious cow is any method, means, or belief that started out as a revelation of God, but over time morphed into a dead religious system.

Religion is when we take what God gave us and start depending on the gift instead of God. And religious people are those who lean more on what they know instead of *who* they know.

Religious cows make terrible eating. But most of us are so used to consuming them that we have no idea we are eating road kill. In fact, most of us mistake it for prime rib. Think about it. How many times have you eaten religious cows instead of throwing them out in the garbage where they belong? Religious cows like:

- Thinking door-to-door witnessing is a highly effective tool.

- Striving to "close the deal" by leading a person in the sinner's prayer.

- Attempting to bring Jesus into every conversation, especially when we are helping people.

- Thinking we must know the Word of God inside out before we can effectively love people.

- Supposing Jesus fits into a nice and neat package.

- Assuming tracts are the greatest evangelistic tool. Ever.

- Reasoning that we need to know the Roman's Road and the ABC's of salvation before we can witness to others.

- Believing we should feel like salesman when we share Jesus.

- Deeming God is in a hurry—so we must act now.

- Judging we are not good Christians until we have led people to Jesus.

- Trusting God would never ask us to do something that we don't want to do.

- Reckoning we have a right to be offended by people's beliefs, especially if they don't line up with the Word of God and don't even get us started on their cultural differences.

Odds are, you have eaten at least one of those cuts of meat in the past. But now it is time for far better fare. While the flames on the BBQ will devour every square inch of religious cow, there are three things that the flames will never devour: faith, hope, and love. And love is the most important of the three.

Love is preeminent.

Love is the reason Jesus died.

Love is the answer to homeless people entering the Cosmo Van rejected and downtrodden and coming out dignified men and women.

Love is the reason foot washing can lead to a guy who just wants some socks getting saved.

Love is behind it all.

If you want to start evangelizing—really sharing the good news—all you have to do is start loving people the way Jesus loved. And loving people the way Jesus loved comes from knowing just how loved you are yourself. You'll read all about that in the next chapter.

Born to Be Wild

Who Are You?

It's really important to know who you are. If you don't know who you are, you can never live to the fullest of your potential—to the fullness of God's call on your life.

So who are you?

I'll tell you.

You are the beloved of God.

Think about it. God loves you. He loves you. You are defined by His love for you and His love in you. That's it.

Who you are is not what you've done in your past. You are not your past drug addiction, jail time, divorce, or anything else for that matter.

Mark Neitz knows that. He is one of my best friends in the world. He and his wife, Jessica, run Why Not Now Ministries. They rescue kids from the sex industry in Asia, provide safe homes for those kids to live in, and give people in remote areas the means to water filtration.

Let's just say that Mark is walking the walk. He knows exactly who he is and who God called him to be. He knows why he was born. He loves people really well all because he knows how much God loves him.

But Mark didn't start out that way.

I have known Mark his entire life; our families were friends before I was born. I remember when he and his brother David first got into trouble with dope not long after their father passed away. Mark became a classic user, cooking and selling meth—and collecting guns.

"You were a wheeler and a dealer and could talk your way out of anything. Isn't that right?" I asked him once.

"Yeah. I was a smart-a**"

When he got out of jail, the district attorney labeled him, "beyond rehabilitation and a threat to society," and had argued Mark should serve the maximum amount of years for his sentence in a state prison.

He was in a rehab program for drug addiction when he landed at our church in Redding, California—Frontline Church.

Mark looked different than I remembered when he walked into the church that first time. He was skinny—sucked up—for a 6'1 guy, and obviously recovering from drugs. His entire identity was wrapped up in his past lifestyle of drug abuse, selling drugs, guns, and jail—and he looked like it too. But he loved being at Frontline. There were other old addicts there too, and it felt like home to him. He knew he was safe from judgment there.

Within a short time of us affirming his destiny and calling out his true identity in Jesus, as well being in the presence of the Holy Spirit, Mark was transformed—his quick wit returned and his hard exterior melted away to reveal a sweetheart who loved Jesus…and then I asked him to be trained as a pastor.

He later told me, "I couldn't believe that someone believed in me enough to want to train me as a pastor. I couldn't believe in me enough… The fact that someone else had Father's thoughts about me before I did was big."

"So, what made you finally realize who you are?"

"Well, after my pastor training, I began to preach sermons I heard you preach. You know, those sermons that called out the gold—or re-affirmed who the hearer was in Christ—in the listener."

I nodded and Mark continued, "And as I preached those sermons again and again at the rehab home I was a leader in, they were cemented in my heart. Slowly but surely, I began to discover just how much Jesus loved me and how much He thought of me. My core identity began to shift from that of an addict to that of a beloved son."

His new identity stuck. Within a few years of being let out of prison, Mark was leading outreaches and mission trips, was ordained, was preaching on a regular basis, and was put in charge of our men's rehabilitation homes.

For Mark, these events were a second chance at life. Always at the back of his mind was the reality that he could still be sitting in jail "beyond rehabilitation and a threat to society" instead of serving the Lord as His beloved, living a life full of destiny and promise.

If Mark had never discovered who he was, he might still be on the streets selling drugs and contemplating shooting the police. He might think that is actually who he is—Mark the addict. But because he believed—slowly at first—that he is Mark the beloved son, the child rescuer, the pastor, the husband, the father…he became all of those things.

And now Mark is living life to the fullest.

He discovered what he was actually born for. And nothing—not his past or anything else—is going to hold him back.

Romans 8:31-32 says,

What then shall we say to these things? If God is for us, who is against us? He who did not spare His own son, but delivered Him over for us all, how will He not also with Him freely give us all things.

The Son of God willingly suffered and died in our place because of His great love for us. But sometimes we forget how phenomenal that really is.

For many of us, it can be hard to truly grasp the magnitude of this sacrifice because we have an enemy who continually tries to convince us that we are not worthy of so great a gift. It's true that, aside from Jesus, we are not worthy, but the greater truth is that with Him we are *made* worthy.

Lonnie understands what it means to be made worthy—he knows what it means to have his identity firmly rooted in Christ. But like Mark, when I first met Lonnie, he was fresh out of prison. When the police had originally arrested him, he had a gun by his side. He had to decide whether he was going to give himself up or go down shooting the police. He decided to give himself up. And he landed in jail.

I showed up on his doorstep with a friend to invite him to Frontline Church, which was barely a month old, soon after his release.

I knocked on the door, and a scowling Lonnie opened it. Everything about him personified "rough." His shirtless torso was covered with tattoos, and he had a hardcore gang vibe. I thought he was going to kill me.

After a few minutes of talking about the church, I suddenly began to prophesy over him, "Dude—you have a serious call on your life." He looked back at me like a cow looking at a new gate.

"All your life you've been running. And you know you're a preacher." His eyes were wide as saucers now.

"I want you to come to our church and be on our team."

Lonnie nodded and told me he was in. I was elated. I knew he was supposed to be with us; I knew from the moment I saw him.

What I didn't know was that there was a backstory.

In prison, God had begun speaking to Lonnie and calling him back home. But Lonnie struggled to believe what he heard God saying. He told me later, "I could not believe that God would accept me or want me back in His house or part of the Kingdom of God—because I was basically a failure at everything I had tried to do, including the most important things like being a son, husband, father. I was massive failure at trying to be a Christian. So I was having trouble understanding why God wanted me at all."

In the midst of that, God also began to tell Lonnie that he had a project waiting for him. That project turned out to be me. When I showed up on Lonnie's doorstep and began to call out his destiny and true identity, a fire was lit in his spirit. Lonnie felt the Lord tell him to commit himself and be a soldier for His cause right then and there. The rest is history.

Lonnie immediately got involved in our ministries—he jumped right in to loving the kids, the helpless, and the hopeless. His tough guy look was a cover-up for a giant teddy bear. But as his responsibilities increased, he felt like he needed to share his past with me. I stopped him in his tracks and said, "I don't care about your past. I care about your future. We value you—you are a vital part of our team!"

I had no idea the impact those words would have on Lonnie's life.

When we were talking recently, he told me the moment I responded to him that way was the beginning of a major shift in his life, "It was such a different response than I was used too—I was valued. I began to realize I was created for so much more; my identity was shifting. I started to see my worth and the plan God had for my life."

"The more I loved the unlovable and poured myself into the people on the streets, the more I realized that I was loved, and that I was not a failure. I began to realize my identity came from Christ Jesus, my savior. Not my past. It's not about what I did. It's about what He did…When you get your identity back, you get your purpose back, and then you know what you are supposed to do."

Now Lonnie is the pastor of a wonderful church in Sacramento. His goal is to reach out beyond the four walls of the church and touch the brokenhearted and the desperate. His church goes after people's true identity and points out their beauty to show them who they are in Jesus. They have a ministry just for bikers. Dark places and scary people don't stop them—they go after everyone—because they think people are worth it.

WHO'S YOUR DADDY?

When we know that we are beloved sons or daughters of God— then we know our purpose. And when we know who we are and what our purpose is, miracles happen and Heaven invades earth. On the flip side, if the enemy can make us think we are less than who we are, then we will not receive the destiny God has for us, nor become the powerful Christ-like men and women God longs for us to become.

In Matthew 4, when Jesus was tempted in the desert, three of the four temptations had to do with His Sonship. The devil started his conniving temptations with the phrase, *"If you are God's son…"* calling into question Jesus' very identity.

If the greatest enemy of our souls would test Jesus, the Son of God, about His Sonship, how much more will he attack our identity as sons and daughters of God?

In order to rule, a prince must know who he is and who his dad is. Of course, the enemy does not want us to rule, so he aims his arrows at the core of who we are. A prince will not rule if he believes he is a defeated, worthless son despite the fact that he is really in fact a prince destined to reign.

The result is that a lot of people are wandering around with major identity issues. They have no clue they were born for more.

Breakthrough comes only when we realize that God the Father absolutely adores us. Believe me, I know. I didn't always know who I was either. And it caused more than a few problems. You'll see what I mean as you keep reading.

ALL IN THE FAMILY

I grew up in a wonderful family. I had two loving parents and three siblings—Bill, Jacque, and Wendi. I was third in line.

My dad, Earl Johnson, was the pastor of a great church called Bethel Church in Redding, California. We were there every time the doors were open.

I loved it.

On many Sunday nights, we had guest speakers—missionaries, prophets, teachers, singing groups, and evangelists. Back then, in the late '60s and early '70s, having prophets come and minister in your church was not as well accepted as it is now. My dad and mom lived with a zeal for more of God, and they pursued Him in every way they could.

I'm going to be honest though: When the missionaries, prophets, and teachers spoke, I caught up on my sleep. I was just a kid. But when the evangelists spoke? Well, I was wide awake! Nothing excited me as much as listening to the stories of people being saved and delivered, as well as watching the miracles that would happen as the evangelists ministered. Even from a young age, the call to evangelism stirred in my heart. It made my boat float.

Being a pastor's son was a lot of fun—there were perks like meeting all of the guest speakers and traveling to new places with my parents.

I never realized that we were in a "fish bowl" for the world to see. I was oblivious to the ways in which other people monitored and criticized our family because of my dad's leadership role.

Nevertheless, my dad and mom never transferred any of the issues or difficulties of their adult lives and the ministry onto us. Even during difficult financial times, we thought we were rich.

They made our lives extraordinary. And I'm so thankful.

Sweat and Tears

I remember being twelve years old and visiting my grandparents house in Willmar, Minnesota. I crawled into my bed late one night not at all interested in going to sleep.

My parents were Pentecostals, and I had a very specific picture in my head of what a "Holy Ghost moment" should look like. And on this night, I was determined to have one for myself—so I started to pray. Really hard.

Unfortunately, I wasn't getting any results that resembled what I had seen in church. So I tried even harder. I know that God loved my heart, but I bet He couldn't help laughing at my determined efforts. I must have looked like a constipated believer trying to give birth to something. Looking back, it was pretty hilarious.

In the midst of it all, in my grandparents guest bedroom, I prayed this prayer, "God I will do anything that You want me to do…except be a preacher. Amen!"

God heard the first part—"I will do anything."

That statement sealed the deal.

He didn't need to listen to the rest.

At the time, I didn't realize that *anything* means "anything" to God. Go figure.

So I continued through junior high and high school with the belief that my "anything-but-a-preacher" prayer had put God and me on the same page. My family had nine generations of pastors, both on my dad's and mom's sides of the family, including my dad and older brother.

I remember thinking that there were already too many preachers in the family. Though I had felt the call to ministry since the age of two, I didn't give it much of an ear. I poured my life into basketball instead. I liked basketball. By nineteen, I was studying to be an engineer at Shasta College in Redding, California. I loved math and anything related to it, and I had pointed my life in that direction because I thought God had heard the second part of my "anything-but-a-preacher" prayer.

I was wrong.

At that time, Redding was a hotspot for Christian concerts. My brother, Bill, and his wife, Beni, were overseeing a street ministry in Redding called the Salt House, and because of their passion for the lost and love for music, they brought in many of the top Christian musicians of the era.

The night when Keith Green came to town forever changed my life.

I remember exactly where I was sitting at the Civic Auditorium. Keith didn't sing a lot that night; he mostly beat us up with his words. I guess you could say that Keith beat the "hell out of me" that night—literally. But the hell I was living in was not rebellion or sin, but rather a wrong mindset and a refusal to embrace my call.

I don't remember exactly what Keith said. All I know is that before the meeting I didn't want to be a preacher, and after the meeting, all I wanted to do was be in ministry. All of the truths that I had learned and experienced as a child and youth in my parents' church flooded back into my soul in a moment. I was set free.

That next Monday at school, I met with my school counselor, changed my major, switched a couple classes, and prepared to transfer to Bethany Bible College the next year.

It's funny, but from the age of twelve to the age of nineteen, I was determined not to become a preacher. Then in one night, God changed my heart. He gave me a taste of my destiny, and I said, "Yes" to the call. However, I still had no real idea what it meant for me *personally* to be a preacher. I still did not really know who I, Bob, was.

For some reason, I didn't remember the people—primarily the evangelists—who I had loved as a child. I didn't recall the life I had felt listening to their stories and observing their ministries. And I didn't connect those experiences to my own destiny.

Instead, I did the next best thing.

I patterned my life and college major after two of my heroes—my dad and my brother, Bill. They were my examples and my mentors. My dad was a gifted counselor and pastor, and Bill was a phenomenal revelatory teacher. I figured that because we were related and because I had learned so much from them growing up, I must have a similar call. So I went to Bible College and got a degree in counseling.

Those who know me personally will understand how much of a joke that is.

True counselors have a special gift to walk with people through their difficulties no matter how long it takes. I am not a counselor and never will be. We evangelists want it done now! I found the whole process frustrating, and even when I did end up helping a person, I still felt like taking my frustration out on someone by the end of it.

Revelatory preaching was likewise not my gifting.

Nevertheless, those were the models I knew, and I strove to imitate them to the best of my ability. It took me years to realize that I wasn't Bill or my dad and that God had a destiny for me that was totally my own. And as long as I was trying to look like someone else, I continued to miss out on what God had planned for me.

UNLEARNING

During my years of Bible College, I dreamed of working for my dad, who was still pastoring Bethel Church in Redding. When Bill had finished school, my dad had taken him under his wing, and I figured the same arrangement would be perfect for me, too.

However, while I was still in college, my dad left his pastorate and took a position at the district office of our denomination.

Suddenly, my dream of working for my dad went up in smoke. I had no idea what to do. Then, right before graduation, Bill drove down to Santa Cruz and asked me to work with him in Weaverville, California, where he was pastoring a small church. I was completely taken by surprise. Weaverville was such a small community and the church was small. I assumed that Bill would not have any need for an associate.

I didn't think it was even a possibility.

However, when he surprised me with his invitation, it took me all of two seconds to pray about it. Working with him meant working with one of my heroes. I could not have imagined anything better.

In May of 1984, I graduated from school and moved to Weaverville within a month. I began working for Bill part-time as his associate pastor at Mountain Chapel. I also worked part-time at a local gas station for Kris Vallotton. After putting in my time at both places, I began to work for Bill full-time, helping out with administration and other aspects of pastoral work.

Looking back, I see now that it was pure grace on Bill's part to tolerate me.

I was fresh out of Bible College. I was like a teenager on steroids.

I thought I knew *all* of the answers.

I later found out that I didn't even know the questions.

One day, Bill graciously told me that it would take me at least five years to unlearn what I had learned in college. At the time, I had no idea what he was talking about.

I do now.

It wasn't that the college I had attended was bad or that the teachings were wrong; Bill just knew it wasn't right for my DNA. The prophetic statement he made that day was pretty accurate— except that it took me more like fifteen years to unlearn it, not five.

Sometimes I'm slow, but I promise I'm worth waiting for.

Because I had majored in counseling, I let Bill know of my extensive expertise, and he began to give me some of his counseling load. What a gracious man. Unfortunately, our arrangement didn't work out very well.

For example, one particular couple came to me because they were having marital problems. After a while, I got tired of listening to their complaining, so I asked them if they were tithing.

They said, "No."

I responded, "No wonder you are having problems. You are cursed, that's all." Then I asked them if they were reading the Bible.

Again, they said, "No."

"How dumb can you be and still breathe?" I asked them, in all seriousness. I told them to start tithing and read the Bible—and then to come back and see me. Needless to say, they didn't come back, and they continued to have problems.

I think you are starting to see why I never should have majored in counseling.

I don't remember the exact date when it began, but in the midst of this, a change started to happen in my life—a change through which the Holy Spirit was guiding me toward my true calling.

Eventually, I began leading the Mountain Chapel youth group, which caused a rebirth of my call to evangelism and the beginning of me finding my true identity in Christ. I started to understand that Jesus loves me just the way I am. And that He made me different than my father and brother.

The young people and I began having early morning classes in my office, where we would study the Word and learn about evangelism. The youth group's theme verse was Romans 1:16, *"I am not ashamed of the gospel of Christ, for it is the power of God to salvation for everyone who believes, for the Jew first and also for the Greek."* We took this verse literally and began traveling the globe—Mexico, China, Russia, Europe—telling people about Jesus; it was glorious.

For the first time, I was beginning to walk in my destiny.

After about ten years in Weaverville, I found myself dreaming about planting a church. I started hanging around more evangelists and gleaning everything I could from them, further developing my call, and in my heart, I felt like it was time for me to run with it. Two of these heroes, who became good friends of mine, were Tommy Barnett, from Phoenix, Arizona, and Bill Wilson, from New York City. I devoured everything I could from them. I even patterned my church plant after their ministries.

OWNING THE CALL

In 1995, while all these desires were swirling in my head, I was sitting in a district meeting for our denomination with my dad, and God clearly spoke to me to start a church in Redding. After the meeting, I told my dad what God had said, and he told me that the district had already been considering planting a church in Redding.

I told him I wanted the job.

Not long after that, I was in Redding, living out my call as an evangelist with a team of like-minded Jesus-leaking people.

We bought buses. Eleven of them to be exact. And we ministered in jails, juvenile halls, hospitals, convalescent hospitals, prisons, streets, crack houses, brothels, and any other place where darkness could be expelled. We had a Sidewalk Sunday School truck, an Ice Cream truck, a BBQ trailer, a baptismal tank on wheels, and a thug bus.

The thug bus was seriously cool. It could convert into a stage. The side of the bus would fold down, and the top would fold up. Little did we know that we had started the transformer era of the nineties.

Along with our thug bus came our thug band, which would perform "saved" versions of songs from the world. We took popular rock songs and saved them, basically rewriting the lyrics to fit the gospel message. Because these songs were familiar to the people we ministered to, they would instantly come and listen, only to discover, as they were listening, that the words were full of life and power—

not full of death and hopelessness as they had been before. For example, we saved George Thorogood's song, "Bad to the Bone," and we rewrote it, "Saved to the Bone."

We drove our fleet of soul vessels wherever there was darkness. There, we would set up and, within a few minutes, would be winning the lost.

It makes me salivate just writing about it. I could write a whole book about our time in Redding; it was mind-blowing.

However, God had something else planned for me—I wasn't meant to stay there.

Two months after I planted the church in Redding, something strange happened. God put the city of San Francisco in my heart. I was at another denomination district meeting, and I distinctly heard God say, "I want you to do in San Francisco what you're doing in Redding."

I didn't know what to think of that.

I had only just started in Redding, and to me it just didn't make sense.

Then, as I was leaving the meeting, I ran into one of the district officials. As I told him about what was happening in Redding, he said, "You ought to think about doing that in San Francisco."

I was floored. Clearly, San Francisco must be important in my life. But I didn't know about the timing, so I put it on the back burner and focused on the breakthroughs that we were seeing in Redding.

Three years later, my friend Bill Wilson was speaking at our church. His message was another pivotal moment for me. He symbolically handed me a running baton and said, "Who will take my place?" Though Bill's ministry was in New York City, I knew that God was speaking to me about San Francisco.

Before that meeting, I had no plans to move to San Francisco. Our ministry in Redding was growing, and astonishing things were happening; yet suddenly the season had shifted.

It was time to move.

In San Francisco, I joined forces with evangelist Mario Murillo, and he began to mentor me—and has been doing so ever since.

On the streets of San Francisco, this gift and call of evangelism was honed in my life to become what it is today. My team and I spent twelve years ministering on the streets and in the projects, feeding the homeless, reaching out to the prostitutes, and loving on all kinds of people. We also raised up other ministries who are doing the same sort of ministry in San Francisco and around the world.

I was doing what I was born for. And I found my identity in the process.

Now that I am back in Redding, I look back on my twelve years in the city with so much awe at what God did. Not only did he allow me to participate in transforming lives, but He transformed mine in the process. I found out what I was born for.

I found my calling as a modern day liberator—I love to set people free, from presidents to poverty stricken children. I discovered I love to sit with drunks on the sidewalk and break bread with people held up in the highest of esteem. My place is not inside the Church. It's on the street. And with my lovely, compassionate, co-pilot, partner, and best friend—my wife, Kimberly. And occasionally in the woods hunting with my brother, Bill.

HOMEWORK

If you struggle with issues of identity and knowing who you are as a child of God, I want to help you conquer this thing—if you're willing. But no one can force you to believe the truth. You must choose to embrace it, just like Mark and Lonnie.

Right now, I will give you some easy tools that will help you get started on your journey toward the truth of who Father says you are. But it's like homework—you have to do it or you won't learn anything.

Romans 10:17 says, *"Faith comes from hearing and hearing by the word of Christ."* In other words, there is power in our confession. We train our minds to believe the words we speak. To paraphrase Matthew 21:21, "If you have faith, you will not only do what was done to the fig tree (command it to wither), but if you say to that mountain, 'Be taken up and cast into the sea,' it will be done for you."

Our spoken words carry great power.

And spoken scripture is especially powerful and encouraging when we are struggling with our identity. The next time you forget who you are, read the following verses to yourself out loud:

Father, I thank You that You formed my inward parts and You knit me together when I was in my mother's womb. I confess that I am fearfully and wonderfully made. I am a wonderful mystery as if embroidered with various colors. How precious and weighty are Your thoughts of me, how vast is the sum of them all (Ps. 139:13-18).

God the Father so loved me that He gave His only son for me (John 3:16).

I am loved by God (Rom. 1:7).

I am more than a conqueror through Him who loves me (Rom. 8:37).

I am a new creature in Christ (2 Cor. 5:17).

I am God's workmanship (Eph. 2:10).

I am alive with Christ (Eph 2:5).

I am an overcomer by the blood of the lamb and the word of my testimony (Rev. 12:11).

This is powerful stuff.

Take an hour and write these verses and others that stand out to you on index cards; then begin to speak them over yourself daily. If one negative word can wither a fig tree, what can a thousand positive words grow? These words can literally transform the way you think about yourself. Remember what happened to Mark as he preached those sermons again and again? Imagine how your life might change if you spoke these truths from the Bible over yourself every day.

The potential impact is beyond imagination.

Here's the truth: You are the beloved!

You are a child of God, an heir of God, and a joint-heir with Jesus. All of the rights and privileges that come along with that belong to you (Rom. 8:16-17). God has a special plan for your life, a plan beyond anything you could possibly imagine. He doesn't see your past. He sees your future. And it's good. Repeat that a few times a day and watch your royal blood start to show. If you want more, just Google, "Who I am in Christ."

That is your true identity.

My greatest desire is that you would come to know the loving, gracious, and merciful Father and how He feels about you. When you discover this, you will be ready to give the world a taste of Father's love. Nothing on earth compares to the joy of participating in this flow of love from Heaven.

It's what you were born for.

Are you getting this?

If so, you are prepared to go on the radical adventure of loving like Jesus loved. However, if you are struggling to understand your identity in Christ, I suggest you camp out right here for a while. Meditate on His love for you until it begins to resonate inside the city of your soul.

It's okay if it takes some time.

What matters is taking the time you need to begin to hear Heaven's heartbeat for you. When you can hear it, then you'll be ready to hear His heartbeat for others. Father always knows exactly what key will unlock someone's heart. He knows exactly what people need. You'll read more about that in the next chapter.

Bungee Cords & Roses

Nash's Story

"Okay son, what are you going to bring?" I looked down at Nash, my ten-year-old son.

His big eyes—keenly observant as usual—sparkled back at me. Whenever I looked at those eyes, I always heard the words, "old soul" rattling around in the back of my mind. That was Nash to a T. He was an old soul.

"Bungee cords." He answered.

Bungee cords. I nodded, knowing that Nash was one of the most sensitive people I'd ever known. If he heard "bungee cords," he heard "bungee cords."

I would always tell my team to ask the Holy Spirit if they should bring, purchase, or do something for that special "one" the Lord was sending them to that night before we would go out. The Lord often uses a simple gift, action, or word, to break open the hardest walls and heal the most wounded hearts. We are always looking for the "one," and we are always asking the Lord what we can give or do or say to find the treasure in that one.

We went to a hardware store and picked up a set of brand new bungee cords and soon we were on the streets looking for the person God wanted us to find that night and give bungee cords to. Several hours passed before Nash pointed her out to me—an old woman pushing a dilapidated stand-up cart piled high with boxes.

Nash nudged me, "Dad…" he motioned with his eyes. "She needs bungee cords."

I watched from a distance as my son made his way up to the old woman. I heard him say faintly, looking into her eyes, "Ma'am? God told me to give these bungee cords to you." He handed her the cords and she started to cry as I watched, the invisible witness from the sidelines.

Those bungee cords had stirred up something deep in her spirit. I couldn't hear what was said next, but I saw my son lay his hands on her and pray for her, tears streaming down her face. He wrapped his hands around her and hugged her like he would hug his grandmother. She hugged him just as hard back, and then she slipped off into the night pushing her cart and boxes now securely fastened with bungee cords, still wiping her eyes and marveling that God knew what she needed.

It was a divine appointment with bungee cords.

Divine appointments like that serve as a sort of heavenly bridge between the Holy Spirit and the one God has His eye on. When we are obedient to do exactly what God says (like bringing bungee cords along on a walk through the streets) God will move. Obedience and "ears to hear" pave the way for a real God encounter unlike any memorized five-step one phrase fits all ever could.

If Nash had gone up to that old woman and asked her if she knew Jesus, the odds are that she would have just walked away. But Nash didn't do that. He had a direct assignment from God to give her bungee cords. He followed through, God showed up, and that woman left not only with bungee cords, but also with a kiss from the Holy Spirit. Nash's obedience looked like and acted like true love because it was. People respond to love. People love to be loved. And our assignment is to love.

Here's the deal: God knows exactly what we need and when we need it. He knew that woman needed bungee cords, and the fulfillment of that need opened up the door for a Jesus encounter.

EXACTLY WHAT THEY NEEDED

Every person Jesus ministered to received a different—*personal*—taste of Heaven.

And by the way, when I use the word *Heaven*, you can interchange it with Jesus, because Heaven and Jesus taste the same.

When the children came to Jesus, the disciples told them to get lost, but Jesus reprimanded His disciples for thinking that way. Then, as He blessed the children, He told His disciples, *"…unless you become like these, you have no part with Me"* (Mark 10:13-15).

I often envision Jesus getting down on the ground with the children and being a jungle gym for them to climb on, not unlike my dad was with me, and how I am with my kids. Jesus knew exactly what those kids needed—a Father's hug and a Father's unlimited time.

Jesus always met people exactly where their needs were.

Lazarus didn't need to be healed. He didn't need to be comforted with the Word. He was dead. He needed life, and that is exactly what Jesus gave him (John 11:1-44).

The blind man didn't really care about a revelation of truth; he just wanted to see. When Jesus gave him his sight, he received such a revelation of truth that he began to challenge and teach the religious elite (John 9:1-34).

The five thousand hungry people had listened to the teaching of Jesus for quite some time without food. Jesus, seeing that the crowd was hungry, gave them food for their stomachs, multiplying one boy's five loaves of bread and two fish (John 6:1-13).

The lady who was caught in adultery didn't know what would happen when the religious leaders brought her to Jesus. She knew death was just around the corner. After all, the law said that a woman caught in adultery should be stoned to death. Instead, Jesus stooped over and began to write on the ground. By the time He had finished, all of the accusers were gone (John 8:1-11). Jesus was the best defense attorney, judge, and jury of the day.

When the disciples needed to pay the Temple tax, Jesus sent Peter out to catch a fish, instructing him to look in the fish's mouth, where there would be enough money to cover what they owed (Matt. 17:24-27). He was the best ATM machine ever.

In all of these instances, Jesus knew exactly what people needed in order to experience Heaven, in order to get a taste of Him. When He met them where they needed Him, they were restored to life, healed, set-free, and delivered. But it took Jesus giving them what they needed—and listening to what Holy Spirit was saying they needed. His three years of ministry can be summed up in the phrase *bringing Heaven to earth*. My brother, Bill, has written a book on this—*When Heaven Invades Earth*. If you haven't read it yet, you should read it as soon as possible. It will radically change your life.

We are called to be just like Jesus. We too are supposed to listen to the Holy Spirit and meet people right where they need to be met most. When we do that—compelled by love and moving on the heartbeat of the Spirit to give people a taste of Jesus—radical things happen. Heaven actually shows up.

One Hundred Roses

Several years ago, I was in Brazil with my brother, Bill, and Randy Clark. We were doing healing crusades throughout San Paulo, Brazil. Approximately fifty Christians had joined forces to bring the good news to the city. There were many meetings, and we spent a lot of time praying for the sick and watching God beat up the devil.

I loved it—but I was also getting a little bored. Our entire ministry was contained to the four walls of the Church, and as an evangelist, I'm not wired to work inside. I need to get outside and get dirty in the streets.

I'll never forget my dad seriously looking at me one time and stating in a low voice, "Bob—never leave the streets. When you leave the streets, you've lost your edge."

That voice came back to me as I sat in my little hotel room I had been instructed to stay in—as, "the streets were too dangerous for foreigners."

Stay in the safe walls of the church and the hotel? That is a dumb rule. I thought. After all, I had ministered in some of the toughest places in the US. Besides that, I was desperate; I needed to find some lost people on the streets. Eventually I decided I was done waiting—it was time for a breakout session. I told Bill and Randy what I wanted to do. They encouraged me to go for it, I gathered a team, and we were off.

San Paulo was not unlike most big cities—sprawling, crowded, and not particularly clean. Poverty was rampant and there was plenty for us to do. While we were out, we met some Christians who were also ministering on the streets. I asked them where I could find some prostitutes. They are easy to find in America, but for some reason I was having a hard time finding them in Brazil.

I am a justice man. God has planted in my heart a deep desire to see prostitutes set free and healed. We often ministered to prostitutes in San Francisco, handing out roses and giving them a father's blessing—letting them know how much their Father in Heaven loves and adores them. We had seen tremendous breakthrough through those simple acts of love. We wanted to do the same thing here, but we didn't know where to start.

After inquiring about where the prostitutes were, we found out that in San Paulo, prostitutes don't roam the streets. They are kept in designated buildings. Our new friends went on to inform us that they had a special ministry just for prostitutes.

This was perfect!

"Can I go with you?" I asked them.

Kindly but firmly, they said, "No."

"Why?" I asked. I didn't want to let this opportunity get away. I was itching to pour out Father's love on the broken.

"We never have men go in to minister with us," they responded.

I understood their hesitation, so I began to tell them about the work that I was doing on the streets of San Francisco. When they heard my stories, it didn't take a lot of convincing—and our new friends agreed to take a few of us into an eight-story brothel the next day.

My next priority was finding a florist. When I did, I ordered one hundred roses. Not surprisingly, the owners of the flower shop were very curious about what I was going to do with all of those roses. I tried to explain it, but it seemed like the more I explained, the worse it sounded.

"Really," I said, "I am going to give them to prostitutes to let them know how much God loves them." It was the truth, but understandably, it was a little hard for them to swallow.

The next day, I took five newbies—who had never done anything like this before—and we picked up the roses, met our new friends, and headed to the brothel. It was an older building several stories high. There were large rooms with eight to ten girls and smaller rooms with one to two girls (the smaller rooms made the girls feel vulnerable and scared, and were less safe).

Starting at the top floor we went into every room, gave roses, and through an interpreter, looked each woman in the eyes and told her about Father's love for her.

In one particular room, we encountered a young girl who was experiencing her first day on the job. She was being trained by a girl who had been there for some time. Like we had in all the other rooms, we prayed for them and declared a blessing over both of them. Later, we were overjoyed to find out that the young girl left the brothel that day and never came back.

We gave out all one hundred roses—and there were one hundred encounters. Heaven showed up in the brothel that day.

As we were leaving, I noticed that the women who had brought us to the brothel (our new friends who ran the ministry to the prostitutes) were crying.

"What's wrong?" I asked, worried I had upset them somehow.

Through tears, they said, "We have witnessed a miracle today. Before, we never allowed a man to go in with us because the curse that was put on these girls came from men. But today we saw another man come and take away that curse."

Get Busy Loving

Listening to Father's voice and doing what He says to do—what He's doing—is what is important. I didn't see the Father going to that brothel and setting the captives free, but I knew that loving on broken prostitutes is the sort of thing He likes to do. I wasn't obeying a divine command from Heaven. Rather, I simply wanted to get out and get busy loving people with Jesus' love. I recognized the need. I knew that He loves those women and that He is always faithful. But because I didn't hear anything specific from Father in that instance, I simply acted upon the truth of Scripture—*"Go into all the world and preach the gospel…"* (Mark 16:15). And in response, Father showed up. He used my desire to spread His love, and He set up divine appointments along the way because He loves those women much more than I do. The rest is written in Heaven. Lives were changed that day, and a curse that had been put on them by men was broken off of them by another man—Jesus in me.

Of course, you don't have to go to a brothel to give people a taste of Jesus. You can be sitting in a coffee shop—like I am as I write this chapter—and give people a taste of Him. As you seek Father and spend time with Him, you will start to see opportunities all around you to love like Jesus loved.

Use Words Only When Necessary

My goal in life is to give people a taste of Jesus. And that's going to look different for every person. Thankfully, the Spirit of God, who lives inside of me, knows the exact needs of each person I talk to—like bungee cords, for instance. I may have no idea what is going on in their lives, but He does.

And as I simply go about life, I am giving the people I encounter a taste of Jesus without even realizing it. That's what happens when you are full of God's love—you unconsciously leak it onto the cashier, your neighbor, your child's teacher, and your mom.

Saint Francis of Asissi once said, "Preach the gospel at all times and when necessary use words."

We are so used to interpreting preaching to mean the proclamation of the good news with the spoken word. Actually, we have the ability to preach more loudly by simply letting who God has made us to be on the inside come out by living out Heaven's love through our actions. Luke 17:21, says, *"...the kingdom of heaven is within you."*

Certainly, our words have power. Using words or not using words isn't the point. I am simply stating that many times the most effective manifestation of God's power flows out from our actions.

The Law Student

During our Night Strikes, before venturing out onto the streets, we always made sure to pray for each one of our homeless friends at the plaza. One night I noticed that a couple of my homeless friends didn't have anyone praying for them. I looked around until I saw a young man I assumed was on our team who was just standing around. I walked over to him, grabbed his arm, pulling him toward my homeless friends, saying, "Come over here; I want you to pray for this guy." And I motioned toward a middle-aged man.

But here's the thing; this kid wasn't with our group.

I had assumed that everyone who showed up at that time of night and didn't look homeless was a part of our ministry team.

Wrong. He was an agnostic foreign exchange student studying law at Hastings Law School—up the street. He had been studying late and was on his way home when he saw all of the people and stopped to see what was going on.

Of course, I didn't know any of this—I was just happily directing my "team." But for some reason he kept quiet and he ended up going out with one of the teams to minister on the streets that night.

When that team came back, he found me and said excitedly, "Earlier this evening you grabbed my arm, and when you did, something came inside me." His eyes were glowing with excitement. He continued, "What was that?"

"What?" I'm sure my face said it all. I had no idea what he was talking about.

He looked at me again and said, "You grabbed me right over there, and when you did, something warm came inside and something cold left. What was that?"

"Huh?" I responded, still trying to figure out who this man was and what had happened to him. He was looking at me intensely and once again he tried to describe to me what had happened, "When you grabbed my arm, something evil left me, and something good came inside. Please tell me what happened?"

"Oh," I responded. "That was the Holy Spirit!"

"What is that?" he asked. That's when I had my first inkling this guy wasn't a visitor from a local church.

I began to explain what was happening to him, and within a few minutes, the agnostic was an agnostic no more. My new friend, who thought he was just passing through, actually was being set up to receive an encounter that ended up changing the rest of his life. He met Jesus as Lord and Savior and was baptized in the Holy Spirit by the time the night was over.

The interesting part of this story is that, when I grabbed him, I didn't feel anything come out of me and go into him, but *he* did.

The Kingdom of Heaven that lives in us is constantly in contact with people every day of our lives. Sometimes we know when this happens, and at other times, it just happens. We must never underestimate the power that resides in us. The truth is, we are leaking Jesus everywhere we go.

When we begin to discover this power in us, we will also start to see the impact it has on those around us. As Acts 4:13 says,

> *Now when they saw the boldness of Peter and John, and perceived that they were uneducated and untrained men, they marveled. And they realized that they had been with Jesus.*

Start taking note of the impact that you have on people. You don't need to change anything that you do during your day; just ask the Holy Spirit to show you the impact that you have on this world and how the Kingdom inside you changes people and circumstances around you.

In the passage above, the rulers of the Sanhedrin came to the conclusion that the only explanation for what was occurring was the fact that Peter and John had been with Jesus. People will come to the same conclusion when they interact with you. They will say, "This one has been with Jesus!"

There is nothing I want more than to be known as the person who has been with Jesus.

DRIVE-BY'S AND BUMP-AND-RUN'S

After a day or two of recognizing the Kingdom in you and the effect it is having on people, you can take an active part in what Holy Spirit is doing. Holy Ghost drive-by's and bump-and-run's are great ways to do this.

So what exactly is a Holy Ghost drive-by?

Jesus modeled one in Luke 8, which tells the story of the woman with the flow of blood who reached out and touched the hem of Jesus' garment.

When Jesus asked, *"Who touched me?"* everyone around Him denied touching Him. Peter tried to explain to Jesus that everyone around Him was already touching Him because they were all crowded together.

Jesus responded in essence, "No, you don't understand; somebody touched Me with expectancy."

No longer able to hide, the woman made herself known and admitted to touching Jesus, testifying that at the moment when she had reached out and touched His clothes, she had been instantly healed. Somehow, she knew that if she could simply touch His clothes, she would be made well.

That woman understood two important realities—first, that the power of God's Spirit is greater than any obstacle; and second, that she could have that power by simply touching the hem of His robe. We have the same power through the Holy Spirit living inside of us. When we catch this reality, it will forever change the way we live.

Bump-and-runs, which are similar, can be defined as "life being transmitted—either accidentally or intentionally—from me into the person I physically touch."

Most of us have no clue that we are participating in bump-and-runs continually through the day. You know that woman you accidently ran into in Target—it was actually God-ordained. Or that new client you shook hands with? When you shook his hand, God shook his world. Whether we are giving attention to it or not, we are spreading encounters with Jesus all day long.

Of course, when we realize that, then we can begin to intentionally bump-and-run too.

And you don't need to add anything "Christianese" to these encounters. We are not meant to lace our lives with "Christianese." We are meant to emanate Jesus through every single thing we say or do or think. That's what a Holy-Spirit drive-by or bump-in-run is all about.

As I mentioned previously, we have been trained in the Church to add "Jesus loves you," "God bless you," and other Christian-sounding phrases to our acts of kindness. At their core, these phrases are powerful, but I think a lot of times we use them out of a sense of obligation.

They are not secret formulas to ensure our effectiveness. Rather, it's Jesus who lives inside us who transforms lives. When we get this, something as simple as giving someone a compliment releases the Kingdom.

WHOSE ARMOR?

By now you may be thinking thoughts like these:

Do I have to be in a good mood for this to work?

What if I am having a bad day?

Does that stop the Kingdom flowing from me?

Or maybe you are wondering, *What if I'm feeling lousy about life and my face looks like I have been baptized in pickle juice?*

Okay, while those feelings may seem like deterrents to releasing the Kingdom, the truth is that Jesus' presence in us and through us is not an on-and-off switch that we control by our moods, or anything else for that matter. We do not have to "act" or "feel" any specific way in order for God to use us.

God made all of us as originals, which is wonderful! But the sad truth is that many of us die as copies. Most of us have tried very hard to become like our heroes rather than searching to discover who we are as unique individuals. One great bonus to living with the conviction that the King inside us changes everything around us is that we get to be real.

For a long time, I tried to become like my dad and my brother.

As you might guess, that didn't work out well for me. I needed to discover who God made me to be—not who He made my dad or my brother to be. Thankfully, when we discover the Kingdom within us, we are able to remain originals. We get to be real: who we were meant to be all along.

Saul tried to convince David to wear his armor, even though it didn't fit him (1 Sam. 17:38-40). In the same way, many believers try to mimic those who influence them or other successful people. They copy their disciplines and methods, hoping to find success, but what they don't understand is that those things are not what God has asked them to do. It's what He asked their *mentors* to do. However, when we discover the Kingdom in us, we will know what we are supposed to do. It could be very similar to our heroes, or it could be very different. The bottom line is that God will highlight those disciplines that will help us to be who God created us to be.

Certainly, God still hones and disciples us to build character, but He does it within the freedom of our unique personalities and calls. He loves who He made us to be—and He wants us to live free.

Many of us have lived with a sense of guilt about the struggles we face. We are afraid to let people see our weakness and shortcomings because we think it will lessen our impact as Christians.

Wrong.

The truth is: If we are passionately going after Jesus, we don't have to wait until we have "arrived" or are perfect like Jesus before we can be a part of giving people a taste of Him.

Know this: *He is constantly working through you, so be free to be you. You are His workmanship, a masterpiece in the making.* Everywhere you go today, preach, and use words only if necessary.

GOOD LEAKS

Before this chapter ends I want to give you a few pointers on how to be a good leaker. They are as follows:

First, when you are interacting with someone, listen, look that person in the eyes, and tell your brain to be quiet. Make a genuine attempt to listen actively.

Second, don't try to give an answer; be an answer. If it is in your power to do so, help the person. Give practical help, prayer, or a prophetic word of encouragement from God.

Third, don't forget that you are an ambassador from another Kingdom, and people are watching, not to condemn you, but to receive from you. They notice something different about you. When you understand this, your expectancy changes.

Fourth, spend time with Father; when you do, you will know what He likes and where He likes to hang out.

Fifth, you have more power than you realize, and you have more influence that you think. Ask Father to give you His understanding of who you are. Look for people who need an encounter with Jesus; then ask Father what they need. When He tells you, give it to them.

And sixth, care for people. Ask Father to give you His compassion for people. You will be forever changed. Certain strategies—like drive-by's and bump-and-run's—will improve your ability to genuinely leak Jesus on the world around you. But it's important to remember that these techniques are designed primarily to stir up the gifts inside of you; they are not "holy" methods to study and copy like a textbook. The goal should always be to allow the Holy Spirit to stir you up and to enliven your heart with His passion for His kids.

The above tips—which are foundational to ministry—may seem obvious; unfortunately, they are so obvious that many people miss them. You are a walking encounter with Jesus. As you release a taste of Heaven everywhere you go, you will be amazed by what happens.

My Hero

There is only one hero who I want to pattern my life after: Jesus.

I could go on forever about who Jesus is to me, but right now, I want to highlight how Jesus gave people a taste of Heaven. He had an uncanny way of reaching people *wherever* they were.

He didn't try to convince them of something.

He simply met them and gave them a taste of Himself.

Every person He came into contact with experienced Him in a different way because He knew their hearts and ministered to them accordingly. Jesus didn't have a formula or a method that He used to help people; rather, He listened to His Father, moved in obedience, and ministered outside of the box.

The Bible tells us that Jesus only did what He saw the Father doing (John 5:19). That doesn't mean that He waited around and copied everything the Father did. Through relationship, Jesus came to know His Father and His Father's heart. He was moved with compassion toward people because He saw them through His Father's eyes. That was the origin of all of His miracles.

Jesus was one with God and moved as such. Jesus recognized the fingerprints of His Father; He recognized where the anointing was. When He saw it, He went after it with everything He had. We are supposed to do the same thing.

If we want to touch people with Father's love, it is vital that we also become one with God so that we can move according to His heart.

So what exactly is God doing? Well, with God—*who* He is lines up perfectly with what He is doing.

And who is God?

Let's break it down. God is good, and the devil is bad.

It really is that simple. With this understanding, we can see that sickness, pain, hopelessness, poverty, disease, suicide, hate, racism, and anything else that points to death are bad—which means they are from the devil.

Conversely, health, blessing, hope, life, abundance, peace, joy, healing, and all things that point to life are good—which means they are from God. So we know that sickness has the fingerprints of Satan all over it. First John 3:8 says, *"…For this purpose the Son of God was manifested, that He might destroy the works of the devil.*" Jesus came to destroy everything that is bad and wearing the fingerprints of the devil.

Jesus knew what He came for and whom He was sent by. He also saw the nature of His Father as *perfectly* good.

Thus, when He ministered to people, blind eyes opened, deaf ears heard, lame legs walked, poor people had the gospel preached to them, hungry people were fed, naked people were clothed, and dead people came back to life (Matt. 11:4-6). More significantly, He prepared the way to the Father for us through His obedience, dying on a cross as a sinless sacrifice for our sins.

Obedience paves the way for true freedom, healing, and deliverance.

Listening for what God is telling you to do and then doing it—whether that is giving an old woman some bungee cords or a prostitute a rose—is obedience.

And obedience opens the door to an all-consuming love with no boundaries and a radically powerful gospel with no boxes.

THE CURVE BALL

WARNING

The odds are that this chapter could offend the old religious spirit. It's a risk I was willing to take. I'm asking you to keep reading. Don't stop and throw the book down halfway through. Remember, sometimes God throws curve balls.

BURNING MAN

Have you ever heard of Burning Man?

It is the largest pagan celebration in the world. Every year, over 50,000 people from all over come together to the Black Rock Desert of Nevada to celebrate whatever it is that each of them believes. There are no rules, laws, or boundaries. The best way for me to describe this event is if the famous *Star Wars* bar scene was crossed with a *Mad Max* movie.

Burning Man is not like going to another country; it's like going to another planet.

And it's one of my favorite places to give people a taste of Jesus.

It's like a bad dream. Evil is celebrated. Yet, in the midst of all of the junk, people are desperate, hungry, and seeking answers. In short, it is the perfect atmosphere for God to show up in, and He does.

Obviously, Burning Man is not a squeaky clean setting, and it includes all of the depravity one imagines in such places. I'm going to tell you up front that some of the things I share may be shocking. But no matter what your feelings are, you need to know the reality is that the people at Burning Man desperately need to know Father's love. We go there to be His love. And like Jesus, who loved the prostitutes without compromising His purity, we loved on all kinds of people with all kinds of issues, and yet kept our hearts pure before Father.

I go to this event with a good friend of mine, Cindy McGill, who has a ministry called Hope for the Harvest. We—along with many other believers who come—set up a tent called the Freedom Lounge, a place where seekers can have an "experience." Little do they know that they will be having an experience with Jesus.

Every year, Father gives us specific instructions about how to minister there. One particular year, He told us not to use any of His names, but just to describe to people what He does. So instead of referring to Him as God, Father, Jesus, or Holy Spirit, we used names such as spirit guide, truth, creator of the universe, energy of Heaven, healer, deliverer, and so on.

Personally, He told me not to introduce anyone to His Son until He said to. My job was simply to give them a God-encounter.

"Then how will they know the encounter is from You?" I asked God.

He responded, "In everything you do, do it with love. My love in you cannot be imitated, counterfeited, or copied. They will know because of your love."

Wow. That took my breath away. What a liberating moment! It's incredible to know that as I genuinely love people, they will know the love comes from Jesus. And thankfully, moments of revelation like this never stop. Father is always upgrading our software.

During that Burning Man festival, some of our team members would staff the tent while some would go out and walk around the playa—the twenty-five square mile makeshift city that is erected in two days and houses over 50,000 people. We would walk from camp to camp, stopping to minister wherever we saw Father moving. Our first day out, it rained pretty hard.

Refreshing.

But messy. The playa dust immediately turned to cement-like mud that added about four inches to the bottoms of our shoes.

A few young girls were struggling to ride their bikes through the sludge, and one of the team members and I asked if they needed us to carry their bikes to their camp. They said that would be very nice, so we picked up the bikes, placed them on our shoulders, and starting walking in the ridiculous mud.

Unfortunately for us, they didn't know exactly where their camp was. It took us about an hour to find it. They were so grateful, and the leader of their camp, who was only about twenty-five years old, also thanked us profusely.

We chatted with her for a few moments, and she asked what our theme camp was. Many of the people come to Burning Man in theme camps, bringing services, food, and a myriad of things that are unmentionable in this book.

"Our theme is freedom." We explained and went on to list some of our services: spiritual readings, redefinement, dream interpretation, organic spiritual alignment, original root recovery, healing with sound, heart transformation, pathway illumination, and so forth.

"Can I have a spiritual reading right now?" she asked curiously.

"Sure," I said.

I slugged over to her through the mud and asked if I could look into her eyes. When she said "Yes," I took a moment and listened to my Father. As I did, God gave me revelation about her life, her struggles, and her fears, as well as her gifts, her future, and her hope. And as I shared with her what I had seen, Heaven showed up.

The woman began to cry and melt before the creator. At the end, she gave me a long hug, through which the anointing was being released even more, and then we said our goodbyes and went our separate ways. It was a very powerful time—and yet during this entire encounter, I did not mention any of the names of God. I only described what He does.

Several days later, a buddy and I were walking from camp to camp when a young woman—who was topless—came up to us and offered us some salad. At Burning Man, you cannot sell or purchase anything. It is all about sharing with one another. So we gladly accepted the young woman's salad, and my friend, who is a dazzling magician, showed her some card tricks. Now I just want to remind you again that Jesus ate with prostitutes and tax collectors without compromising his morals or sinning. Our hearts were clean before God.

About ten minutes after we had left the young lady, Father gave me a very specific word for her. I said, "Okay, Father, if you want me to give her that word, You will have to bring her into our path again." Remember, there were over 50,000 people in a twenty-five square mile radius. Nevertheless, if He gives me a word for someone, He can arrange our divine encounter. And sure enough, a few days later, we ran into this same young woman again, along with her boyfriend. I asked her if I could give her a spiritual reading.

"Oh, please!" she answered.

But right before I was about to give her the word, God downloaded a powerful prophecy for her boyfriend into my heart.

"Can I give him a reading first?" I asked, pointing to him.

She nodded and I looked at her reluctant boyfriend. He agreed hesitatingly and listened as I shared the word. All of a sudden, he broke—the words had pierced his heart.

For this couple, the words from Father created one of those changed-forever-in-a-moment kind of encounters. They received an absolutely stunning taste of Jesus. But once again, Father did not want me to mention His name or His Son's name; I was only allowed to describe His character.

You know what?

That was really hard to do.

I wanted all of the people I encountered to know who was responsible for these life-changing events, but I was obedient and I bit my tongue, wondering what Father was planning.

Throughout that week, we had many divine appointments in which hungry people encountered the love, grace, and mercy of Father. We saw lots of healings and miracles; some people were instantly delivered, and others received powerful words from Heaven that forever changed their lives. And still, I did not have permission to introduce anyone to Jesus.

Okay. I realize that hearing these stories may make some people want to debate theology with me. If you are one of those people, take a deep breath. I want you to know that my goal is simply to express that we were obeying the instructions Father had given us, whether we understood them or not. They did not contradict Scripture (i.e. we weren't claiming God told us to commit adultery or be involved in lewd acts), but they did violate our understanding of Scripture (i.e. the urgency of telling everyone about Jesus this instant). We were confused too—but we were obedient. We knew God had a secret plan up His sleeve, and we were excited to see what was going to happen.

Got it? Good. Now, keep reading.

THE FRUIT OF OBEDIENCE

After a week of these sorts of encounters, we reached the last day of the festival, which turned out to be a little different. We started out the day like we always did, with prayer and worship; we were having a wonderful time in the Lord. On previous days, as soon as we had finished our prayer time, some of us would venture out onto the playa to minister from camp to camp. On the last day, Father had other plans; before we had even finished our time with Him, people started to pour into the tent to receive ministry. Something was up. We immediately divided into teams and began to minister.

I began to talk to a young man who, as we discovered after a bit of prayer, had several demonic guests that day.

To be honest, I don't particularly enjoy praying for those possessed by demons. I want the anointing Jesus had with the Gerasene demoniac hanging out in the graveyard (Mark 5:1-20). He simply told the legion of demons to go, and they went. Usually, in my experience, these encounters with demonized people take a while. I was glad I was paired up a friend of mine, Mike Norton; he loves doing that kind of stuff. And together we prayed, found the root, and got those suckers out.

When the young man was finally clean, I heard my Father say, "Introduce him to My Son."

After eight long days, I could introduce Jesus.

Now I was really excited.

I gave our newly delivered friend the gospel story and boldly told him that he needed to ask King Jesus to come into his life.

To my surprise, he just stood there, unresponsive, with his eyes closed.

I waited a minute and then repeated myself, thinking maybe he hadn't heard me and I needed to speak a little louder.

Again, he stood there, still as all get out.

I looked at him and said loudly, "Buddy, we just got rid of over fifty demons; now you need to fill yourself with Jesus so those things don't come back and you can have a victorious life!"

In a soft voice he responded, "I know."

Then, like thunder, he lifted his hands toward Heaven and shouted, "YESHUA, COME IN!"

It was as though time stopped. God came with power and knocked the young man off his feet. Later, when he came to, we found out that he was Jewish. Now he had become a Jewish believer in Jesus.

Then I looked around the room and saw a young woman. I heard the Father say, "Go and tell her about My Son."

I walked over to where she was being ministered to, knelt down, and asked her to look into my eyes. Then I asked her to forgive me on behalf of all the men who had hurt and used her. Tears came down her face as she spoke forgiveness; then she embraced me. In that moment, I became the father she had never had; it's hard to put into words the power of healing that happened in that embrace. I then asked her if she would like to know that same love that she had experienced as she looked into my eyes and embraced me, in her heart.

"Please." she said.

So I told her how much Father loved her and that He bankrupted Heaven just for her. Immediately, she grabbed my hands and asked Jesus to come into her heart. She had found her Father, and the love she had encountered that day would no longer be a momentary experience, but a constant reality.

Already, my heart was filled with joy.

As soon as I would finish with one, I would hear the Father say, "See that one over there?"

"Yes."

"Tell that one about My Son."

"With pleasure!"

Nine people received Jesus as Lord and Savior on that last day. At a place like Burning Man, the fact that nine lost children found their way home is an absolute miracle. It remains one of the biggest miracles that I have ever seen, heard of, or had the privilege of experiencing.

So what happened?

Why did Father keep us quiet about salvation for so many days?

Honestly, I don't know. As Psalm 115:3 says, *"…He does whatever He pleases."* I believe, however, that the salvations we experienced on the final day were a direct result of our obedience on the seven previous days.

As I said before, those seven days were not easy for me. I wanted to share about Father with every person I met—but the Holy Spirit held me back. At times I almost felt blind, even though we were seeing many remarkable things happen. But even though we didn't understand why, we were still faithful. As a result, He gave us the favor, anointing, and privilege of leading many to Him that last day.

OFFENDED?

When we walk with Jesus, we will have plenty of opportunities to be offended.

Jesus did a pretty good job offending the religious leaders, and even His own disciples, during His life on earth.

What makes us think He won't ever do anything that offends our understanding today? He is the same yesterday, today, and forever (Heb. 13:8).

People—intentionally or otherwise—are good at offending us too. There are plenty of other believers doing things that, for whatever reason, we don't agree with. Yet sometimes they have fruitful lives, or even ministries. At times, we will observe questionable "fudging the line" situations that bother us. We often encounter ideas and situations that we don't understand and others that we can't even begin to wrap our minds around.

So what do we do? How do we avoid becoming offended? How do we stay open to the creative and occasionally perplexing moves of God that do not line up with our idea of how God should move?

We must acknowledge that *there is no box*. God is God, and He is good. He will do what He pleases, when He pleases.

The Church cannot afford to be offended.

Ever.

Look at the fruit of the offending idea or method. Only good trees produce good fruit. Even if the tree is not producing (in our opinion) good fruit, we must remember that we are not called to pray judgment on others.

Ever.

Instead, we are called to pray for grace and blessing. After all, that's how we want other people to pray for us, right?

When we lack understanding or something just simply bothers us, we must release the grace and blessing of our Father to the people involved. God did not make you or me the sheriff for His cause. Instead, He gave a promise, and that promise is the Holy Spirit. It is the Holy Spirit's job to convict the world of sin, righteousness, and judgment (John 16:8).

Judging people, talking badly about them, or harboring offense in our hearts is not our job—it's His.

Our job is to love one another.

KOSHER

Kosher. No shellfish, no hamburgers, or clam chowder for that matter.

Eating kosher was a key part of being Jewish. It was perhaps the very thing that separated Jews from Gentiles. It was the "separateness" that made God's chosen people stand out. Every little Jewish boy and girl was told what to eat and what not to eat. They were told that what they put in their bodies made them spiritually clean or unclean. It would have been unfathomable for a good Jewish man or woman to eat "unclean" food. It would have been close to blasphemy.

I've personally always loved Acts 10. It takes kosher to a whole new level. In this passage, Peter is praying. He is also hungry.

All of a sudden, he falls into a trance and sees a large sheet from Heaven being lowered to him. On the sheet are all the things that, according to Jewish law, he is not allowed to eat.

Then he hears a voice from Heaven saying, *"Get up, Peter, kill and eat!"* (Acts 10:13).

His response is immediate, *"By no means, Lord, for I have never eaten anything unholy and unclean"* (Acts 10:14).

I'm sure he thought it was a test, being hungry and all. Surely the Lord wouldn't want him to eat such things. Then the voice came again *and said, "What God has cleansed, no longer consider unholy"* (Acts 10:15).

This happened three times.

Apparently Peter needed things done in threes in order to get the point across.

I am like that sometimes, too.

As Peter ponders the vision, the Lord tells him that three men are waiting for him downstairs and that he should go with them. Long story short, an angel appeared to a Gentile man named Cornelius and told him to send for Peter so that he could receive the gift of the Holy Spirit. Peter goes, and for the first time ever, the gospel is preached to Gentiles.

In the midst of Peter's message, the Spirit falls on all the Gentiles in the house, and they were filled with the Spirit before they were even baptized as believers (Acts 10:34-48).

This was a turning point in history.

Through these supernatural events, the leaders of the Church were challenged to change their belief that salvation was only for them—the Jews. God didn't care anymore whether you ate a cheeseburger or a Philly cheese-steak. *Everyone* could have the Holy Spirit. The vision was about way more than food though. It was about people. God was making the point that He cared about the heart. Of course, he cared about the heart all along, but that seemed to get lost in translation for a lot of Jews. That is why He put Peter in a trance and told him, *"What God has cleansed, no longer consider unholy"* (Acts 10:15).

Isn't it interesting that God placed unclean food in front of Peter when he was already really hungry?

God loves to use our circumstances—like hunger—or emotions to communicate deep truths or revelations. Sadly, so many believers live life stunted because they are convinced that God is not an emotional being. The truth is, God is an emotional being, and He made us in His image as emotional beings.

He understands our emotions and our physical bodies, and He will use what He needs to in order to get our attention—just like He used food to speak to a hungry Peter.

THE ILLUSION

I realize that the heart of this chapter could be easily misunderstood. Some may think I am pushing the envelope too far for the sake of the gospel. Some may think I am glossing over sin or removing absolute standards.

I can assure you I am not.

I believe in absolutes, and I believe the Bible. I believe in sin and in Hell; I believe in salvation through Christ alone, and I believe in Heaven.

Nothing I have said contradicts those truths.

What I have done is question some of the ways that we traditionally interpret the Bible and interact with sinners. So many times we rely on our own brainpower or the same old tools instead of relying on the greatest tool—the Holy Spirit. Tommy Barnett, a great evangelist and pastor I love and respect, instilled this belief in my heart, *"The method is not sacred; the message is."* When I first heard him say those words, they revolutionized everything I had ever thought about evangelism or the Christian life in general. That phrase has shaped my life.

We try to fit into a box of evangelizing and we get stuck, frustrated, or just plain bored because nothing happens. The box just isn't working for most people anymore.

But here's the thing: There is no box to begin with.

The box is an illusion.

It doesn't exist now, and it never has.

How could you fit inside—or outside for that matter—something that does not exist?

You can't. When the only method you follow is that of following the Holy Spirit, you will never feel trapped in a fake box again.

It is impossible for God to fit inside anyone's box, even my "no box" box.

I know there is no box, but I also know that He is much bigger than my "no box" illustration. God will do what He wants when He wants to whomever He wants, all because He is God. Think about Psalm 115:3 again, *"But our God is in the heavens; He does whatever He pleases."*

It's hard to argue with that.

God loves us so much that He bankrupted Heaven for us (Rom. 8:32). In Acts 10, He violated His own law by telling Peter to get up, kill, and eat stuff he earlier said not to.

Think about it: He was the one who established the law about not eating anything unclean in the first place. Jesus became the fulfillment of the promise and the acceptable propitiation for our sins. That means there is a new set of rules. God the Father works differently now.

That does not mean that He violates Scripture, but it does mean He will sometimes violate our *understanding* of Scripture—all for the sake of the gospel.

And the truth is: He asks some of us to do things that would offend a lot of the Church.

The key to understanding our role and responsibility in evangelism is realizing that we are called to inspect the fruit, not judge the caretaker of it. The Bible makes it clear that, as believers, we are not to judge other people (Matt. 7:1; Luke 6:37; Rom 14:13). But we are told to judge the fruit of other people's lives and ministries so that we can know how to sow our time and money. Jesus said that only good trees can produce good fruit (Matt. 7:17-18). In other words, we will know the condition of people's hearts by inspecting the fruit of their lives. And how can we know the fruit of their lives?

It's simple: Answer these two questions.

Are souls being saved?

Are people experiencing Father?

The answer to those two questions should clear up whether the fruit is good or bad.

So often, we judge people or ministries based on their method rather than by looking at the fruit. We get caught up in being offended by what others do that is different or makes us uncomfortable. But that is doing it all backwards; Jesus told us to look at the outcome—not the method.

I'm not saying that we should be so open-minded that our brains fall out, but we need to understand that God works in many different ways and that He works through imperfect people.

None of us have a perfect revelation of the truth. And we simply cannot afford to be offended and miss out on what God is doing through others just because their methods look different from ours.

Our eyes must be on Jesus. We need to know what He is asking us to do. And then we need to do it. We do not need to worry about anything else.

And when we focus on Jesus, He gives us keys and strategies for individuals that have the power to change cities.

That's exactly what happened to us in San Francisco. God gave us a key to the heart of a love-starved city. We let go of all our boxes and we allowed Father to lead. The results were astonishingly sweet. And I can't wait to tell you about them.

What a Transvestite, a Food Truck, & a Widow Have in Common

Father's Heart

The Tenderloin—an area in downtown San Francisco known as a hotspot for prostitution, drugs, violence, and a large homeless population. I learned early on in ministry that my light shines brightest in the darkest places, and so the Tenderloin is where we decided to start our ministry after our move to San Francisco.

One evening, as I walked the streets, the main question that kept revolving around in my mind was, "What is the key for this city?"

Father's response was so tangible it was as if He wrote the words in the air in front of me. "Treat Hell's trash like Heaven's treasure, and love the children. Then I will give you the city."

The words burned into my heart and my spirit jumped. He had given me more than just a practical assignment; He had also given me keys to the city of San Francisco. And when God spoke that assignment to me, my team and I ran with it, always dreaming with

Father of how we could treat the homeless, the prostitutes, and the throwaways better than we did the day before. There was limitless potential to this simple, yet profound San Francisco assignment of loving people the way Father does.

How could I more powerfully show the love of my Father to those the enemy has thrown away?

How could I be a more accurate picture of Jesus with skin on?

If I gave them sandwiches one week, what could I do next week to make it better?

The list of hopes went on and on. Dreaming with God became a large and crucial part of walking out my assignment—and it still is today. Whether I was walking the streets of the Tenderloin or visiting another city, I would dream about how I could carry out my assignment better than I did the day before.

When I was a child, I would often enthusiastically share an idea with my parents. Without fail, they would respond excitedly and positively—even if it wasn't a great idea. I do the same thing with my children—it brings me joy to hear their thoughts, their hearts, and their dreams.

Our Father treats us the same way when we dream with Him. He loves to hear our ideas, and He is excited about every one of them because He's excited about us.

I think that's why dreaming with God is one of my favorite activities.

Nevertheless, I personally find it difficult to dream when I am busy or running hard after my goals. Dreaming is not some mystical, spontaneous thing that just happens to me. It's actually the opposite. I have to make a deliberate effort to dream with God. This goes beyond "quiet time" with him, while not reducing or taking the place of its significance. Dreaming with Him is tapping into the possibilities of Heaven—and it is rooted in relationship.

Relationship is built on the everyday mundane aspects of regular old life and realizing that God is present through *all* of it. For me, this usually looks like having my eyes wide open and looking around while having a conversation with Father.

From this place, we go into dreaming mode—together.

BEGINNINGS

I want to share a story with you. It's a story of a dream come true. And I think it fits as a perfect illustration of how dreaming with God can have some pretty incredible results.

It all began as I stood against the Orpheum Theater in San Francisco and looked around at the United Nations plaza, watching the people who had come out to treat Hell's trash like Heaven's treasure with us on the streets. It was a pretty cold night, and I rubbed my hands together as a feeling of joy welled up in my heart.

This was a good night.

Some of our people were sitting with a drunk-out-of-his-mind homeless man and were pouring out the love of Jesus on him.

Others were giving out clothing. Watching the looks on the faces of those receiving the garments was priceless.

A few more were releasing healing or prophetic words to those in need.

At the food table, some faithful ladies were serving soup, fried bologna sandwiches—an experience we should all have at least once—peanut butter and jelly sandwiches, and juice or coffee.

As my wife would say, my heart was happy. And so was Father's.

"Isn't this cool?" I said to Papa.

"Yes, it sure is." He responded.

Now remember, the San Francisco assignment was always at the forefront of my mind. Because of that, every time we set out to do something new, we would first ask ourselves, *Are we in line with our assignment?*

With that in my mind, as I was talking with Father that night, I began to dream, "Wouldn't it be cool to feed our homeless friends fried chicken, mashed potatoes and gravy, pan-fried corn bread, fresh vegetables, and homemade cake?"

"That sounds good!" He responded.

I don't know if you know this, but Jesus was a southern Jew. Serious.

I began thinking, *We are seeing tremendous breakthrough with what we are doing right now. We are seeing healings, salvations, and deliverances. We are feeding our friends sandwiches and soup, but what if we fed them a hot meal— the sort of meal Father would serve them? That would really tick the devil off, and we would be taking our mandate to a whole other level.*

I was always looking for ways to do what we were doing with more excellence. This certainly fit the bill. The more I dreamt about it, the more excited I became—and I felt God getting excited right along with me. And as our dream expanded, it suddenly hit me— what we needed was a food truck.

"Why don't we build a kitchen on wheels, fully equipped with everything we need to make that meal happen?"

I could sense Father's smile as He said, "That's a great idea; let's do it!"

The Manna Truck dream was born. And it was born out of me leaning against a wall, feeling amazed by what I saw people doing for Jesus, and talking to Him about it.

The Manna Truck

In Habakkuk 2:2, it says *"Write the vision and make it plain on tablets, that he may run who reads it."* When I went home that night, after dreaming with Father, I wrote down everything we had dreamt about. I included all of the details about the truck and the appliances and equipment that it would need so that we could cook these delicious meals.

Then I began to tell people about the dream. Sometimes you need to share a dream if it is going to become a reality.

And the more people I told, the more excited I became.

This dream had been born out of my intimacy with Father. He and I dreamt it up together, and because of that, I couldn't even hear the naysayers. When we have a God-dream, no person, demon, or circumstance can discourage us because it was born in His presence. When our dreams are born in His presence—out of communion with Him—we will persist until the dream becomes a tangible reality.

When I traveled and preached in various churches, I would share this dream. One particular church caught the vision and raised over $75,000 for the truck. The way God provided was simply incredible. We were ecstatic. The dream was taking shape.

We went ahead and purchased the truck—the Manna Truck, as we affectionately dubbed it—and we found someone who could build it into the type of mobile kitchen I had imagined. We had several meetings with our builder and nailed down exactly what we wanted.

I believe in doing things with excellence, and I wanted to build the homeless a Lexus rendition of a food truck to feed them. I wanted everything to be *just* right.

Finally our plans were finished, and we began to purchase the materials.

Okay, now brace yourself. This is where the story takes a sharp turn. The builder we were working with took our money and most of the supplies, and he took off to who knows where.

We lost everything except the unfinished truck.

How did that affect the dream?

To be honest, it didn't affect my dream. Okay. Yes—I did have to walk through some forgiveness issues toward the man who had stolen from us, but the dream remained intact.

Nonetheless, we still were out of funds, and life marched steadily on. The Manna Truck dream of feeding thousands amazing food served with Father's love—though intact—was now on hold.

A few weeks later, my team and I drove up to Redding, California, to visit my family, and while we were there I stopped by to visit a family friend. She was a widow restricted to a wheelchair due to multiple health issues. At the end of my visit I prayed with her, and right before I left, I asked if I could use the restroom. She smiled and pointed the way.

As I walked to the restroom, I couldn't help but notice how rundown and dirty the doublewide trailer she was living in had become.

When I walked into the restroom, I discovered that the lights didn't work. The floor was a mess, and the toilet was on its last leg. In fact, the trailer was on its last legs. And it concerned me.

I said my goodbyes and got into my car, but I couldn't stop thinking about how rundown her home was. The whole drive home, all I could see was that floor and the toilet, and my friend in her wheel chair. As I hit a red light, the audible voice of God entered my car. Sometimes God speaks very clearly—especially when it concerns how His kids are being treated.

"What are you going to do?"

"Fix it?" I questioned.

I didn't really need an answer. He had seen the floor and the toilet too. She was His treasure. He was not happy about His daughter's living condition. His question was actually a pretty simple and profound order. So the rest of the way home was spent strategizing about how I could fix her run down home.

My sole reason for fixing up her home was simply obedience. God had asked me, "What are you going to do?" And I knew in that moment that He wanted me to give this woman a practical demonstration of His love by fixing her house, so that's what my team and I did. And the truth is, I am pretty sure I wasn't the first person Father had asked to do something about this situation; I was just the one who finally said, "Yes."

At our next team meeting, I told our team the story and asked if they wanted to come and help me. Everyone on the team agreed.

We didn't take a camera or film crew to document our work. It would not have necessarily been wrong to film it, but that wasn't what we did. We were just being obedient and serving someone who couldn't serve us back. Getting people's approval or praise was not part of our thinking.

Let's just say God had mercy on me because we signed up for way more than we could accomplish. Thankfully, He sent reinforcements to help, and in two days, we had totally remodeled—including lowering her oven so she could cook without burning herself—and cleaned the house from top to bottom. And we had spent $3,000 more than we had in the budget.

When the team asked me how we were going to pay for all of it, I said, "Well guys, that's God's department." I honestly was not worried. God had commissioned me to fix His daughter's house, and I knew He would cover the bill.

As we worked, I walked around and told all of the volunteers that Heaven was watching and well pleased—and something great was going to happen as a result. And I totally believed it too. God was going to do something awesome.

While we were doing the remodel, we arranged for my friend to stay in a hotel and be fully taken care of. When she came back home on Monday, tears ran down her cheeks as her daughter wheeled her through her home; she had a new lease on life.

After that, neighbors would come over and ask her what had happened. She would simply respond, "Jesus."

Then they would ask, "Can Jesus do this for me, too?"

God's blessing in her life had a ripple effect on everyone around her. She became a living encounter with Father's love.

THE PHONE CALL

After our weekend in Redding, we came back to the Bay Area and continued ministry as usual. Not long after our return, I received a phone call at our office.

"Hi—Bob Johnson?"

"Speaking."

"Umm—I was in San Francisco last weekend and I ran into one of your team members. He gave me a newsletter about the Manna Truck you are building, and he told me about the cool stuff you are doing in the city."

I thought back…several months before all of this happened, I had sent out a newsletter describing my dream for this truck to our entire mailing list. In the newsletter, I described exactly what the truck would do and how it would release greater blessing and anointing to the city. We had several hundred people on our mailing list at the time, and sometimes our team members would take the newsletters with them when they were doing special events for our ministry. We never knew what God might use to tug on a person's heart.

The woman on the phone continued, "I am amazed by all I have heard, which is why I'm calling. Would you explain the Manna Truck a little bit more to me?"

I gladly told her the whole story about how we wanted to treat the people on the streets even better by serving them hot meals. She sounded very interested, so I told her even more, still unsure about who she was.

After we had talked for a little bit, she told me that she and her father specialized in building that type of truck.

"Wow," I said. That's great."

"I would like to build the Manna Truck for you," she told me.

"Wow! How much does something like that cost?" I asked.

Without answering my question, she began to tell me her credentials, how many people worked in their plant, how long they had been in business, and many other details about their company.

I politely asked again, "How much?"

She responded again with a list of their previous clients—including all of the United States Armed Services, Burger King,

McDonalds, and on and on and on. I knew right then and there that I was being baited and set up for the kill shot.

I said again, "Wow! That's great. How much does something like that cost?"

"You don't understand," she said. "God kept me up all last night and told me that I am to build this for you for free!"

"Free?" I asked, not quite believing what I was hearing.

"Yes!" she reassured me.

I was absolutely speechless.

She then asked if I had plans for the truck.

"Yes, but they are probably not very good," I admitted.

"What about a dream list?" she asked.

"Yes ma'am." I said. That was something I definitely had.

Reality set in as we ironed out the details of how to get our truck to her plant in New Jersey. My friend, Mark Neitz, and I drove for three days straight to take the truck from California to New Jersey as quickly as possible. When we arrived, we met with their engineers, gave them our dream list, toured their plant, thanked everyone so much, and then headed home.

God had completely provided—and not just for any old truck, but for a truck designed by the best in the industry. He wanted His kids fed right.

MOVING HEAVEN

Was it a coincidence that this miracle happened right after we fixed the widow's house?

I don't know.

To me, it seems like the perfect timing of God. I dreamt about building a truck to feed Father's treasures in a spectacular way. I began to work on the dream, but it came to an abrupt halt when the money was stolen. The dream had not died; neither did we put it on the back burner. We continued talking about it and stirring the vision inside as many people as we could, but at that time, we simply didn't have the funds to continue building.

In the meantime, I heard God ask me to bless one of His daughters, and I did. While we were at the widow's house, I believe we truly moved Heaven. When I walked around and told our team that something great was going to happen as a result, I had no idea the impact my declarations would have.

We didn't just fix the widow's house, but upgraded the entire place—and because of that, I believe we touched Heaven to move for us. Father was pleased that day, and He looked at His angels and I imagine He said, "What is one of the dreams that Bob has?"

The obvious reply was, "The Manna Truck."

So He said, "Well, I have another one of my kids in New Jersey who builds those things. Go down and keep her up all night and tell her to build that for him."

What I know for sure is Heaven gave us one *incredible* truck.

It took the company about a year to finish this beauty, but it was well worth the wait. It was a roach coach on steroids, and it made me the envy of every roach coach owner in California.

I wanted to build a Lexus Manna Truck—because we should do everything with excellence for the Lord—but Father gave me a Bentley Manna Truck. His standards of excellence are quite a bit higher than mine. It was truly beyond anything I could have asked for or thought of. I had sown $3,000 that we didn't have into the renovation of the widow's home. In response, God gave us a Manna Truck worth $300,000!

That is a one hundred-fold return.

In the end, my simple dream resulted in tens of thousands of people being fed. Because of that, they tasted Jesus, and they will never be the same again. A lot of people who were treated like Hell's Trash discovered they were Heaven's treasure. When they ate that corn bread, they felt His love. And hundreds of those who have eaten from this truck now have their names written in the Lamb's Book of Life.

We must never think that any dream we have is trivial.

When a dream is birthed while dreaming with Father, it will have eternal impact. Sometimes we won't get to see it until the day when we see Jesus face-to-face, but we can be confident in God's faithfulness. So keep dreaming, keep dreaming, and keep dreaming some more. God is always good, and He loves making dreams come true—especially dreams that demonstrate His heart for His children.

HEAVEN'S TREASURE

Of course, feeding people out of an awesome truck was only one of the many ways we would reveal Father's love while walking out our assignment to treat Hell's trash like Heaven's treasure. A different, but equally beautiful, way was to go out on Friday nights and hand out roses to prostitutes (which is where we got the idea to hand out roses in Brazil). We would give the girls a rose and say, "Just like you see this rose is beautiful, that's how my Father in Heaven sees you. You're a beautiful woman of God. And your Father loves you more than you can imagine."

One particular cold Friday evening, I came across a very young, very beautiful girl. I handed her a rose and asked if I could pray with her.

Immediately, she said, "No!"

In my experience, people on the streets rarely turn down offers of prayer. Being the type of person that I am, I also don't like it when people tell me *no*.

I looked at the corner of the street and saw her pimp staring at her, so I quickly said, "You don't have to listen to me, but let me pray for you."

She said, "No!" with even more fervor.

I knew that Father wanted to do something more than just give her a rose, so I continued, "I'm going to pray for you anyway."

She quickly responded, "You don't get it do you?"

"I guess I don't," I said.

She inhaled and spit out, "God doesn't hear me anymore."

"Who told you that?" I asked quietly.

"The Church."

"Why did they tell you that?"

"I used to be a man, and now I am a woman. That's why He doesn't hear me anymore." Her voice was hard, but behind it was a heart-wrenching sadness that betrayed her brokenness.

"They didn't tell you the truth," I said. "I know that my Father listens to you." I took her hand, lifted my eyes toward Heaven, and said, "Father, come." When I looked back down at her face, tears were streaming down.

God the Father came down from Heaven and wrapped His arms around her.

She said, "I guess He still listens."

As far as she knew, she had committed an unpardonable sin, and God had left her. That was so far from the truth. She needed a God encounter, and she got one that night. I didn't ask her if she wanted to receive Jesus as Lord and Savior.

I wasn't supposed to.

I was just planting seeds of God's love. For all I know, that may have been her first real taste of Jesus.

Not long after, I gave this testimony in a church one night, and after the service, a dear saint came up to me, quite bothered by my story.

She exclaimed, "What did you tell this man to do?"

"What do you mean?" I asked.

She said with a louder voice, "What did you tell this man to do?"

"I don't know what you mean," I said. Okay, I knew what she meant, but I wanted to get a point across.

She said again, sounding quite frustrated, "What did you tell this man to do?"

"I didn't tell *her* to do anything."

I took a breath and continued, "You see, it is not my job to clean the fish; it's my job to catch them."

Jesus said, *"Follow Me and I will make you fishers of men"* (Matt. 4:19).

We are the ones who catch the lost with His love.

Only the Holy Spirit's job description includes *"convict the world of sin"* (John 16:8). Personally, I am glad that's not my job—my job is fun: treating Hell's trash like Heaven's treasure.

Jesus paid for every person's salvation.

He already did it. He sees every single person as a treasure.

Our assignment as believers is to discover Heaven's treasures in the people we meet at school, the bus stop, the grocery store, the mall, or wherever God happens to place us. When God expressed His heart to me for San Francisco, He was expressing His heart for the world.

All people are Heaven's treasures—God's children: from the transvestite to the widow in the run-down trailer to the homeless lining up outside the Manna Truck. Most just don't know it yet. When we treat people according to who they are in God (and not according to their sins), we partner with Father's heart. We open doors for people to encounter Heaven and to step into their destinies as children of God. And we actually see and treat them like God does: as His treasure. That's our assignment—right? It goes way beyond corn bread and roses.

SOME FINAL THOUGHTS

Now that we are nearing the end of this chapter, I want to go over a few things about assignments and dreams that you need to know.

First of all, your initial assignment or dream is only the beginning. It *will* grow—according to God's law within nature that says if a thing is not growing, it's dying. The workmanship of God is always growing.

Nevertheless, it is not enough to have an assignment, a passion for a cause, or a dream. You must have keys and strategies for their success. And it is necessary to pray for these strategies and keys.

Second, your strategy or dream may look like someone else's. Father gave me a similar assignment and dream to two of my heroes—Tommy Barnett and Bill Wilson. Because of that, I structured my ministry after theirs. Now, I want you to know that I did not simply take their models as my own because they were successful. I was not mimicking their good ideas. Rather, their strategies resonated in my heart and God said, "This will work really well for you too—I want you to go for it."

Too often, people copy something that someone else is doing, hoping they can get the same results. The difficult thing with that is that it's not always what Father is telling them to do.

Third, I want to make it clear that I am not laying out a method for you to follow. I am personally committed, wherever I go, to dream with God and to listen to His strategies and timing for that particular place. I have to work hard not to get ahead of or behind Him. The same will work for you.

Yes, that is a method. And it is one of the few methods that I suggest you should follow. Certainly, you are welcome to use any of my ideas that God ignites in your heart. But the key is not the strategy: The key is listening to Father and remembering that every single person is His treasure.

Keep that in mind as you read the next chapter, which happens to be about—of all things—methods.

THE THREE P'S

Picture this: One night, a group of excited young people believing for miracles took to the streets of San Francisco. They came across a bitter Vietnam Vet stuck in a wheelchair who happened to be a friend of mine named Bob. They asked him if they could pray for him and he let them. So they prayed, and the power of God hit Bob.

He literally *jumped* out of the wheelchair.

That night, Bob had an encounter with God, and he was changed in a moment. He met Jesus and received him as Lord and Savior. From that point on, he anxiously waited for us to show up on Friday nights so he could help us set up for another Night Strike.

Thanks to a bunch of crazy young people who went out of their way to give him a taste of Jesus, Bob can walk. Think about it—he couldn't walk before, but now he can. Something like that will change every aspect of your life—not only physically—but emotionally and spiritually as well.

Okay, now let's just be real for a moment. In today's society, words are cheap. And the same accusation is made by many against Christianity. People are burned out on theology and the do's and don'ts of religion. They value *experience* over *ideas*. In essence, they are saying, "Show me your God. Stop telling me all your beliefs about Him; I'm not interested unless I can see what He's like."

So, when God backs up His Word with signs, healings, wonders, and miracles like he did with Bob the Vietnam Vet, it leaves a *completely* different impact than any number of sermons ever could. Heaven-encounters tend to leave people speechless because they penetrate the mind and pierce the heart. And even though onlookers may doubt what they have seen or give a bunch of explanations for why it couldn't, "really be a miracle…" the person who received the touch from Heaven will never be the same.

First Corinthians 2:1-5 says,

> *Brethren when I came to you…my speech and my preaching were not with persuasive words of human wisdom, but in demonstration of the Spirit and of power, that your faith should not be in the wisdom of men but in the power of God.*

The apostle Paul used many methods to preach the gospel of Jesus. I imagine Paul's favorite method was watching God step in and perform miracles for those he was preaching to.

Since my early days in ministry, my focus has changed dramatically from preaching an impressive sermon to actually seeing people changed forever from encountering Jesus. And while I used to want God's power to validate me, now I long for it to free those who are in bondage. I love to pray for people, lay hands on them, and see them healed right before my eyes. One of the desires of my heart is that even my shadow touching people would cause them to be instantly healed. I long for the day when, upon seeing a blind man, I can gently brush up against him, watch the anointing cause his eyes to open, and then quickly slip into the crowd anonymously.

Many of us, if we're honest, are more motivated by the excitement of having God's power work through us than seeing what His power is actually doing. It is easy, when praying for the sick, to be more excited about the manifestation of God's power than we are about the impact it will have on people's hearts and lives.

Jesus was moved by compassion for people. That, and obedience to Father, were His primary motives. It is a subtle difference with *big* implications.

Those need to be our primary motives too.

This is why I long for the mystery and subtlety of God manifested in people being healed, not because I took a step of faith, but because faith lives inside me. This is a different level of hunger for miracles—a hunger deeply rooted in the sort of compassion that Jesus had.

I believe this is where God is taking us, and I believe it is a very important aspect of being Jesus to the world.

This chapter is all about what happens when you usher in Heaven-encounters and miracles. Particularly, I am going to highlight three types of evangelism—power evangelism, prophetic evangelism, and practical evangelism—the Three P's. The Three P's are simple tools you can use to shower Father's love to His lost children.

Are you ready to dive in? I am. And I'll give you a heads up. We are going to start with power evangelism.

Power Encounters

Power evangelism is just what it sounds like: the dynamite power of God demonstrated here and now on earth. Bob's story above is—you guessed it—an example of power evangelism.

I want to share another amazing power encounter: One night during my San Francisco days, my best friend, Mark Neitz, and I were walking down Market Street looking for people to pray for. We had just heard an incredible testimony from a friend, and it had gotten us all fired up. Our friend had seen a man with a broken foot. So, he jumped to the floor, grabbed the man's foot, and commanded order into it—all without asking permission from the man with the injury.

Despite his unusual method, the outcome was awesome.

The man's broken foot was healed. And as it turned out, he was a backslidden believer who came back to Jesus through his encounter with God's power.

That night, as Mark and I were walking, we saw a man with a broken foot walking down Market Street. Mark dropped down to the sidewalk, grabbed the man's foot, and released order to it. Then he got up from the sidewalk, and we walked on without so much as a "God bless you" or anything.

A few moments later, that man began shouting at us. "Hey! Hey you! Hey you guys, stop!"

We immediately turned around to see the man walking toward us, stomping his broken foot on the ground. He caught up to us, arms waving, "There's no more pain! There is no more pain! You guys scare me!"

We didn't try to lead this man to Jesus. We told him that God healed his broken foot because He loves him so much. That was ridiculously fun and extremely simple.

THE TENT

Several years into our ministry in San Francisco, our team was consistently seeing many healings, miracles, and deliverances every time we ministered on the streets. It was not so much that we knew what we were doing, but that *whatever* we were doing was working. We were just doing what Father said to do when He said to do it. And it worked every time. It wasn't because of our experience or expertise, but because of our simple obedience.

In the midst of this, two of my friends, Mike and Bronwyn, came to me with an idea. They wanted to have a prayer tent set up on the streets so passersby could get prayer!

I thought to myself, *We don't need a stupid tent to see God move.* But being the kind, generous pastor I am, I said, "That sounds like a great idea—as long as you head it up."

They were excited, and the very next week they set up their tent in the United Nations Plaza and started praying for people.

It's not that I thought it wouldn't work; I just thought it was a silly idea—I'm being real here. I was standing by the Manna Truck when I heard someone shouting my name. When I looked around, I realized that the voice was coming from the prayer tent. I walked over and found a group of very excited people. Before me stood an older couple; the man was blind, and the woman was crippled. This couple had come to the prayer tent wanting prayer. Our team prayed for the man first, and immediately his eyes opened. His wife was so excited that her husband could see that she literally jumped out of her wheelchair. She was healed too, without any prayer.

BARHOPPING GRANNIES

One of my favorite memories from our time on the streets, and another one I think is important to share here, was the time when Mark and I took some grandmas barhopping. We talked with the grandmas and explained to them what we wanted them to do.

God and Grandmas have a direct line of communication. Everybody knows that. And we decided to take full advantage of that fact. We picked our bar, seated the slightly fearful and unsure grandmas at a table—let's just say they were in a very unfamiliar environment—and put a sign on out that read: FREE PRAYER. It wasn't long until the first person, or shall we say, victim, came up to the grandmas and asked for prayer.

After the first man received prayer, these grandmas transformed right before my eyes. At first, they had been like little puppies; suddenly, they were ferocious dogs, with devil-blood dripping off of their jowls. I could hardly believe my eyes.

"Okay, ladies. Next time, I want you to keep your eyes open and look at the person you are praying for, and when the unction of the Holy Spirit jumps on you, prophesy over him."

"You got it!" They growled with excitement.

Soon another man started to approach them. As soon as he entered the "grandma zone," he started to shake. By the time he reached their table, he was already on his knees. The grandmas wasted no time; they blasted that man with the Holy Spirit.

Meanwhile, Mark and I were sitting at the bar, having a coke and talking to the owner. Nodding to the grandma table, she asked us, "What are you doing with that table?"

"We came here to bless you and your bar," I answered with a smile.

She gave us a puzzled look. "What?"

"We want to release a blessing to you and your bar," I repeated. "Can we do that?"

"Umm. I guess so," she said, still not sure what we meant.

So I grabbed her hand, and Mark and I prayed to release the blessing of the Lord over her and her business. We didn't ask God to shut it down or curse it; we asked Him to bless it. That was an exciting night at the bar as we watched evil leave and the glory of the Lord come.

Power Evangelism

I love stories like these because they show what can happen when we give God the space to move. In essence, that is what power evangelism is—it is giving God an open door to encounter people through us.

Power evangelism happens when we become desperate for God's intervention and provide Him with opportunities to move. If we never expect it, it may never happen. But when we live with expectation and back our expectation up with risk, we will see God encounter people with demonstrations of His love through power, signs, and wonders.

Ask the Holy Spirit to teach you how to move in power and to open your eyes to see the opportunities to do so every day. When

He comes—and He always does—watch to see what He does next. Sometimes He wants to lead people to His Son; at other times, His goal is simply to give people an encounter with Him.

My goal after a power encounter is not the sinner's prayer. Sometimes we think, *How could they not want to follow Jesus after what He just did for them?* The truth is, God is the only one who knows people's hearts and understands what it will take to woo them into becoming totally His.

Now when God reveals someone's heart and destiny to you, it is called a prophetic word. When He reveals their past to you, it is called a word of knowledge. When He tells you to use that information to bless people and pour out His love on them, it is called prophetic evangelism. We are going to talk about what happens when you move into prophetic evangelism next.

Prophetic Evangelism

Let me set the stage. It was a cold night on the streets, and I was ministering with a great friend of mine, Lonnie Nix. Standing across from a famous strip club in San Francisco, we were praying and ministering to different passersby.

Halfway through the night, two young, lower-end prostitutes came along our way. A lower-end prostitute is one who will perform her services for just a little cash or simply for drugs. Both of these girls were on black tar heroin and spaced out of their minds. I approached the first girl and asked her if I could pray for her. She slurred out a "Yes." I asked her if I could hold her hands, and again she complied. I then asked her if she could look into my eyes. She did the best she could.

At that point, Father, in His grace, gave me some insight into her life. I very kindly told her several events from her past that I knew about only because Father showed them to me. These words were laced with grace and hope. I let her know that none of the events that had happened were her fault and that my Father in Heaven really loves her.

At no point in our conversation did I belittle her or instruct her to repent or get right with Jesus—that would not have been treating her like the treasure God declared she was. When I had finished pouring out the love of the Father on her, she dropped my hands, fell to her knees, lifted her hands toward Heaven, and cried out with a loud voice, "Father, forgive me!"

She *instantly* sobered and gave her life to Jesus.

After we were finished praying with her, we walked over to her friend, who was equally incoherent because of heroin. Father gave me insight into this girl's life as well. When I finished, she too dropped my hands, fell to her knees, lifted her hands toward Heaven, and cried with a loud voice, "Father, have mercy on me!" This second girl was completely spaced out on heroin and did not have the ability, in her natural state, to mimic her friend. Her response was a holy moment, as she also instantly sobered and gave her heart to Jesus.

The prophetic is a stupefying key that God uses to open people's hearts so they respond to Jesus. I love it because while not everyone may need healing, everyone does need a word directly from God. Everyone—from the highest-ranking general to the little boy picking through garbage in a Mexican dump—wants to know that God knows their name.

COLT .44

Okay, it's time for another story.

I was pastoring in Redding and Sue—one of the wonderful ladies from our church who ministered every week in convalescent homes—asked if I would come after our morning service and minister at one of them with her. I agreed. When we arrived at the home, we discovered that the nurses had brought in about a dozen of her friends, who were ready to receive the Word.

This was the first time I had preached in a convalescent home, and I was underwhelmed when I realized that all twelve of the people in my audience fell asleep during my devotion.

Apparently my preaching had room for improvement.

After the devotion, Sue asked me to talk with a man named John who she had been trying to reach for some time.

"Sure," I said. "Why not?"

As we walked toward his room, she warned me that he hated preachers and was an angry, cantankerous old man who loved nothing more than arguing.

"Cool. Bring it on." I said, knowing it was a set up for God to do something great.

We walked into John's room, and I attempted to have a normal conversation with him. Apparently he had some sort of prophetic gift because right away he asked me if I was a preacher. When I responded in the affirmative, he began cussing me up one side and down another. He was pretty hostile, and I thought to myself, *Sue wasn't kidding, was she?* I stepped back from the bed and let Sue take over for a while.

I noticed some photos on the wall so I walked over and looked at them. While I was looking at them, God gave me the key into John's heart. I walked back over to the bed and asked him about the photos. He was reluctant to answer because he just didn't like me.

"That's my son and me," he grumbled.

"He looks like a good son," I said.

He nodded. "He sure is."

Then I told him that I had a son, too. (This is where the key that God gave me starts.) I asked him, "Do you love your son?"

"Yes!"

"Yeah, I love my son, too," I said. "In fact, I love my son so much I wouldn't hesitate to die for him."

"Me, too." he said.

"And another thing," I added. "If someone tried to hurt my son, I would kill him and not even hesitate."

Suddenly I had his attention. I'm sure he thought, *Maybe this preacher isn't so bad after all if he would kill someone.* "I would, too," he agreed. "Nobody messes with my son."

I looked at John and said, "Let's say, for story's sake, that your son was here visiting you, and I walked in with a Colt .44 revolver and pointed it at you. As I'm pointing it at you, I said, "John, I'm either going to kill you or your son, but one of you is going to die today."" Then I asked him, "What would you do?"

He didn't hesitate. "I would tell you to kill me, not my son."

"You mean to tell me that you love your son so much that you would give your life for him?" I asked.

"You bet," he said.

I said, "That's true love, sir." He thought for a moment.

Then I looked at him and said, "You know, there is another kind of love I don't understand; I call it crazy love."

"What's that?" he asked.

"I can't understand how anyone would love so much that he would allow his son to die for someone else. That is crazy love."

The preacher-hating, God-denier was about to get a revelation. I continued, "John, that's how much God the Father loves you. He loves you with that crazy, stupid, unexplainable love, and He let His Son Jesus die for you on a cross so you could have a relationship with Him."

Tears began to run down his face. I asked him, "Would you like to receive that love?"

He said, "Yes."

Right there, Sue, John, and I grabbed hands, and he asked Father to give him that love.

The Spirit of God knew everything about John, and He also knew the key to his heart. I later found out that John was a descendant of the outlaw Jessie James, and as a result, he thought of himself as an outlaw as well. God, in His mercy and grace, told me to point a Colt .44 at him and threaten his life.

That was the key to his heart. Who knew?

God did.

The next Sunday, Sue brought me a little piece of paper. It was an obituary. John had passed from this life into the next just four days after he met Jesus. God loves people so much that, even in the final days of their lives, He sets up divine encounters to draw His treasures home.

Nevertheless, as wonderful as my experience with John was, the truth is that moving in the prophetic often does not look anything like my experience in the convalescent home. Sometimes God positions us so that we can be the tipping point in a person's life—as I was with John. But most of the time, evangelism can be summed up in this phrase: giving people tastes of Heaven. That is often as simple as complementing a person on having a beautiful smile.

ARE HORSES FROM THE DEVIL?

One night when my wife, Kimberly, and I were eating out, I looked at the server and heard God tell me that she liked horses. I thought to myself, *Okay. That's kind of weird, but I will go with it.* That was all I heard at the time—horses.

The next time she came over to the table, I looked at her and said, "So you like horses, huh?"

She was shocked. "How do you know that?" she asked.

I said, "God told me."

Immediately she ran away—crying. I looked at Kimberly and said, "Well, that didn't go like I thought it would." I even thought to myself, *Thanks, Father. Now she's probably going to spit in my food.* I know that's a horrible thought, but that's what was in my mind.

The next time she came back, God gave me another word to share with her concerning her hopes for the future. I thought, *Well, here goes nothing. My food is probably already ruined anyway.* I gave her the word and she ran away again—still crying.

What have I done? I thought. *Am I hearing wrong? I better go in for a check-up to see if my hearing is off.*

The next time she came back, I asked her very gently, "Why am I making you cry?"

She told me, "At my church today, I learned that what you just did was from the devil."

"Oh, I'm sorry," I said.

"That's okay," she said, smiling. "At first I was scared, but I thought to myself, *How can this be from the devil? It gives me hope and makes me feel like God loves me.*"

At the end of our conversation, we prayed with her, encouraged her to follow her dreams, and reminded her that God loves her very much.

I want to emphasize that the goal of the prophetic is to give people a taste of Heaven—an out-of-this-world experience. We are not in competition with the so-called psychic world; ours is the true experience. Anything that the enemy uses is a counterfeit—a cheap imitation. He doesn't have the ability to create anything, but only to twist and distort something that God has created and called good. A word from God brings redemption, hope, and freedom. Other words you may receive could be from well-meaning believers, which breathe confusion or hopelessness, or words from the other camp—which breathe death and bondage.

Isaiah 61:1-3 says, and I'm paraphrasing here, that we have the anointing to preach good news, release healing, proclaim freedom, set captives free, release favor, and bring comfort. That's exactly what happens when the Word of the Lord goes forth from the anointed believer's mouth.

THE RISK

Now, I took a risk when I stepped out and mentioned horses to the waitress. But it was a risk that sure paid off. Risk is at the foundation of prophetic ministry. Anytime God gives me a specific word for someone, I have to be the one to deliver that message. It's so easy to start second-guessing and asking, *"What if I am wrong?"* But the bottom line is that we need to be willing to make mistakes.

If our desire to give the word is motivated by Isaiah 61—but we miss the boat or make a mistake—we need to just shake it off. We must not let the enemy talk smack in our ears; he would love nothing better than to make us doubt our ability to hear God's voice. Our compassion for people will drive us to be givers of life, hope, and futures. Sometimes, in giving a prophetic word, we will miss the mark—we're all human, after all—but that's okay. We must persistently shake off the shame of our mistakes (while, of course, learning from them) and look forward for the next time God will give us a word for someone.

The purpose of the prophetic is to set people free, give them hope, and point them to Father. This is how you *will* know if you are using the prophetic properly. Get comfortable with the reality that you will make some mistakes. The key, when you make mistakes, is to get back up and to go at it again. Righteous people, though they sometimes fall, will get back up over and over again (Prov. 24:16).

I strongly encourage you to read books on the prophetic, study what the Bible says about it, and most of all, to take risks in ministering God's love through prophetic evangelism. Kris Vallotton, from Bethel Church in Redding, California, has many wonderful and insightful teachings and books on the prophetic for those interested in learning more about this important tool.

I also want to point out that in order to be effective in prophetic evangelism, we must learn quickly that the person's response to the word cannot be our motivation. Rather, our motivation must be to simply obey God's voice. Getting this right will put us way ahead of the game. I try to never ask people if what I am saying is accurate. Asking these sorts of questions just creates a roller coaster ride of emotions within us related to our worth and performance, and it makes it harder to be willing to take risks when we hear Father speak. Rather, our focus must be on our compassion for people, our desire to see people set free, and our desire to hear the Father's voice.

Okay, so now that we have that covered, it is time to move on to my personal favorite of the Three P's: practical evangelism. Practical evangelism is the heartbeat of who I am. I want you to know that the following stories tell of my discovery of the key to Father's heart. As you read them, I pray that you discover it as well.

Practical Evangelism

Imagine a cool evening in the Tenderloin. Expectancy was in the air, and our usual fleet of soul vessels and Jesus-marine foot soldiers had gathered ready to go out and spread the good news. On that particular night, we didn't have anyone to cut hair in our Cosmo Truck—our beauty salon on wheels. Because no one else was available, I volunteered to do the hair cutting.

I had only cut dogs' hair before.

Here's hoping! I thought as I took my station.

We also had a medic working in this truck, Mike Staneart, who would take care of minor medical issues. Outside of the truck, we were washing the feet of the homeless and giving them clean socks.

The first man who came in said he wanted me to shave his head. This sounded easy enough so I grabbed the clippers and proceeded to cut his hair. I honestly had no idea that those things could actually cut someone's head.

Fortunately he didn't feel a thing because he was drunk.

I quickly washed the blood off, had our medic bandage him, and sent him on his way. However, after that first fiasco, I decided I should just stick to hair washing.

The next person who came in was a good friend who I had met on the streets. Let's call her Mary. Mary was in a wheelchair because she was missing one of her legs. It was obvious that she had a hard life on the streets. She was a heroin addict, and she survived by begging and scavenging.

Every time I saw her, my face would light up, and I would say, "How are you, sweetheart?"

She always responded with a warm smile saying, "I'm good, thank you."

I eventually found out how she had lost her leg—her boyfriend had shot it off with a shotgun several years before.

That night she wheeled up to the truck and asked if I could wash her hair.

"I would love to," I said.

Another one of the team and I picked her up out of her broken wheelchair and carried her to the salon chair. I put her head back in our salon-style hair-washing sink and washed her hair with warm water and lots of shampoo and conditioner. This was a first class experience for our homeless friends, and I could tell Mary was enjoying it. When I was done, she asked if I could wash it twice.

"You bet!" I said. When I finished, I sat her up in the chair and started to blow-dry.

Mary had long, thick black hair; my 1750-watt blow dryer was no match for it. It would take a *long* time for her hair to dry. However, I wasn't about to send her into the night with wet hair because was so cold in the city at night. So there I stood blowing her hair dry.

The next thing I knew, I was having an out-of-body experience. The Bible contains stories of many people who had similar experiences. Don't get distracted by the theology of what *exactly* happened to me; just listen to what God did.

I was transported to Heaven, and all around me, people were walking—laughing and free. I caught a glance of a young lady in front of me, and as soon as she saw me, she came running over to me, jumped up in my arms, and started hugging me. I hugged her back, thinking, *I guess this girl thinks she knows me.* After she let go, she looked me in the eyes and said, "Do you remember me?"

Hesitating, I admitted, "No, I'm sorry, I don't."

"I'm Mary," she said. "Remember the night when you picked me up, sat me in your chair, washed my hair, and told me about

Jesus? It's me! I just want to thank you so much. Because you did that, I'm here in Heaven! Thank you!"

Then, once again, I was back down on earth blow-drying Mary's hair.

Father had given me a taste of what Heaven is going to be like. I had seen Mary there, but hadn't recognized her because she was a young, beautiful girl who had been made new.

On earth, Mary had a very tough life. She was battered and beaten-up. She was an addict; her teeth were rotting, and she had sores all over her body from the heroin. In my vision of Heaven, Mary had both legs and a whole heart. She was deeply thankful for the encounter with Jesus' love that she had while I washed her hair.

I like to paraphrase Matthew 25:34-40 this way:

Father said, "Way to go, kids! Come and receive your reward because you took care of those I asked you to take care of. You fed me when I was hungry, you clothed me when I was naked, you prayed for me when I was sick, and when I was in prison you came to see me."

His children responded, "Father, when did we do that?"

He said, "When you did it to the least of these, you did it to Me. Way to go! I'm so proud of you!"

Practical evangelism is just that—seeing the opportunities all around us and doing what we can to meet the need. If someone is hungry, we take the time to get some food. If someone is sick, we make the time to pray for healing or get them medical treatment; if someone is cold, we give them our jacket. Practical evangelism means caring for the hurting, intentionally looking for those who need a taste of Heaven and giving them an encounter that they will never forget.

S S S

Our Sidewalk Sunday School (SSS) was another way we saw the love of God embodied in people who loved children in the projects of San Francisco. In order to take Sunday School to the streets, we converted a collection of box trucks into mobile Sunday School trucks. We cut one side off and put a piano hinge on the bottom of the side we had cut so that we could open it as a stage. The trucks were then outfitted with sound systems, toys, games, and everything we needed to teach children in the projects about Jesus. Within minutes, in any location, we could set up and start loving children. Thousands of children came to know Jesus as Lord and Savior.

We also had an ice cream truck that would tag along—going into the most dangerous places in the city. It had a special assignment. The only way anyone could get something from the ice cream truck was to memorize the memory verse from the previous week of SSS. So right after SSS was over, kids would line up in front of the ice cream truck ready to recite their verse. Romans 10:17 says, *"Faith comes by hearing and hearing by the word of God."*

We knew that if we could get the Word of God into these children, their lives would change. Often adults from these neighborhoods would also line up for ice cream. When I would walk up to them and ask if they knew the verse, they would assure me that they did, often with colorful adjectives interjected. And they received their ice cream too.

The children we ministered to had no money, so we did what we could to help them, especially during important events. Right before school, we loaded up backpacks with everything that they needed for school that year and had a back-to-school backpack giveaway. The mayor of the city even showed up to help. Every year, we gave out hundreds of backpacks. At Easter, we would hide over 100,000 candy-filled plastic Easter eggs in different parks where the children could look for them. Before they took off to find the eggs, we always told them about the reason for Easter. Christmas time was also very special, and the gifts the children received from us were usually the only gifts they would receive that year.

I often would sit on the blue tarps with the kids as the leaders were teaching. The SSS leaders—Morgan and Chanel—who continue to lead SSS in San Francisco to this day, are absolutely extraordinary. They would do all the work, and I would just enjoy the day with the kids. On this particular Saturday in the projects, as I was sitting on the tarp, a little four-year-old girl scooted over and cuddled up with me. After about five minutes, she looked up at me and said, "Will you be my daddy?"

My hearted melted. Immediately I said, "Sure, I will be your daddy!"

I couldn't take her home with me, but I was able to give her a moment when she had a daddy and she experienced Daddy's love. Moments like that forever change you.

The key that God gave me to impacting the city of San Francisco—treating Hell's trash like Heaven's treasure and loving the kids—was primarily accomplished through practical love. One of my heroes, Heidi Baker, often says, "Love looks like something."

It looks like clothing the naked, feeding the hungry, sitting in the gutter with the vomit-covered drunk man, holding a sixteen-year-old prostitute in my arms in the pouring rain while she told me that nobody loves her anymore, washing the feet of the homeless and anointing them with oil, doing nails for transvestites—all the while telling them how beautiful they are—and continually being the hands and feet of Jesus to all I encounter. That is the beauty of practical evangelism.

What Love Looks Like

Out of the Three P's, practical evangelism is the most simple.

However, in some ways, it is the most difficult, too, because it often requires a much greater time investment than power or prophetic evangelism. Most of the time, a commitment to practical evangelism means being willing to be *inconvenienced*.

I have found that people almost never need help when I have extra time. Sometimes helping other people is extremely inconvenient, but I think that's the point. Practical evangelism is not about being a social Band-Aid or relieving personal conscience; it's about putting hands and feet on love.

That's what Jesus did when He came to earth, lived life as a human, and died on the cross for our sins.

It was hardly convenient.

Love rarely is.

Living as a manifestation of love is a sacrificial choice that comes with an incredible payout. Jesus endured the cross because of the joy set before Him—His ability to have relationship with us (Heb. 12:2). The same is true for us. Our reward is the joy of participating in bringing Heaven to earth and showing broken people how much God loves them.

The Three P's and the stories I have told to illustrate them are just a few examples for you on your journey. Allow the Holy Spirit to take your imagination to new places so that you can see the potential of simply loving people. You may never minster to a homeless person, but God may send you to Wall Street to love on people who are—in their hearts—worse off than the homeless ones.

A soul is a soul, no matter how lost.

Father gave His only Son for all of them, and not one is less or more deserving than another. Rather, the Bible clearly tells us that God's desire is for all people to be saved (1 Tim. 2:4).

Before we go on to the next chapter, I want to make something clear. The whole point of the Three P's is to give a supernatural taste of Jesus by displaying His power, speaking words of love and encouragements, and meeting immediate needs. The Three P's do not have to be packaged so that those you are loving and helping know where it's coming from.

Jesus said it pretty clearly: *"By this all men will know that you are My disciples, if you have love for one another"* (John 13:35).

If the time is right (Father will make that clear to you), let them know how much God loves them. When you truly love people, they will know you are different. They will be able to tell when you don't want something in return. As a result, you are giving people a taste of Jesus. If they taste Him enough, they will never be the same.

Many times on the streets of San Francisco, I prayed for those who needed miracles in their bodies. I prayed boldly in the name of Jesus that they would receive their healing, but I didn't lead them to the Lord. I didn't do it simply because I didn't feel Father release me to lead them to Jesus. Father let me know that they weren't ready to make the choice for Jesus yet. Loving them and giving them an experience of God's power was the assignment for the moment.

When people are ready, they will make the choice for Jesus, and because they are not pressured into it prematurely, they will never turn back.

Our goal in loving people through the Three P's should not be to lead people to Jesus or get them to pray the sinner's prayer. Rather, our goal is simply to give them a Heaven-encounter through love. When they encounter powerful, prophetic, or practical manifestations of God's love, they can't help but be changed. We believers were changed in His presence, and the lost will be changed in the presence too. As Romans 2:4 tells us, *"…the kindness of God leads you to repentance."*

All you have to do is ask yourself these two questions: "Where has God placed me right now?" And, "How can I become love to those around me?"

If you've asked yourself those two questions, and you are where you are supposed to be doing what you are supposed to be doing, you can rest easy. Jesus loves people too much to leave their salvation in your hands alone. Timing is the Lord's. You do not have to worry about leading people to Jesus right now, this instant, if Father is telling you to wait. Your job is to love.

There is no hurry when it comes to love.

You'll see what I mean when you read the next chapter.

seven

YOU CAN'T HURRY LOVE

It was another night in the Tenderloin. I was walking the streets and came across a beautiful young girl who was selling herself. Her eyes darted about anxiously, and I could tell she was desperate, exhausted, and hurting with a pain most of us will never experience.

My heart immediately broke, and I felt the Holy Spirit lead me to go and just talk to her for a little while. She was open to having a conversation, and after a few minutes, I asked if I could pray for her. Embarrassed, she flipped her blond hair aside and quickly said, "No."

"Please let me pray for you," I repeated—you already know that I do not like to be told *no*. Besides, when people say *no* on the streets, there is normally a pretty heavy reason behind it.

But again, she emphatically said, "No."

"Is there a reason you don't want me to pray for you? What's going on?" I asked gently. She paused a moment and then looked up into my eyes.

"I am a pastor's daughter. I am the definition of a failure. I have failed my parents, and I have failed God. Please don't pray for me. I'm not worth it." She was being completely honest.

"Your parents love you very much and so does our Father in Heaven. I know this for sure," I said, "because I am a daddy." The words just flowed out of my mouth. Her eyes began to well up, and then she let me pray for her. The Holy Spirit was there in a mighty way, and as I held her, she wept from the depths of her heart.

I didn't ask God to convict or judge her.

I asked Him to wrap His loving arms around her and let her know how loved she was.

I didn't ask her to repent, and I didn't go through the sinner's prayer with her.

I just held her.

And when she was done crying, I told her how loved she was and that no matter what she has done, Father God longed for her to come home.

She gave me a hug and slipped into the night. For the next several weeks I kept my eye out for her on the streets. But it was as though she had disappeared. I was worried about her.

Finally, after weeks of asking different prostitutes on the streets for her whereabouts, I found out that she had left the streets and gone home to her parents. When I heard those words, I cried.

Father knew exactly what was needed to unlock her heart and turn her back to Him.

It wasn't the gospel message or a call for repentance.

It was a hug and a declaration of Father's love.

Don't miss the message here. Sometimes we do more than what Father is doing, and we mess things up. I could have done what I was trained for and tried to "close the deal" with this girl, but that was *not* what Father was doing.

He was loving a prostitute who felt alone and rejected.

And the result was reconciliation and redemption.

LOVE KILLER

I'm not sure exactly how it happened, but somehow in the Church we ended up with a whole lot of urgency.

Perhaps it resulted from the excitement about who we serve or the sobering reality that many are dying daily without Jesus. Maybe it stems from the popular belief that everything is getting worse and time is running out because we're in the end-times. Regardless, as a whole, we live with a sense of urgency—which translates into stress and pressure.

We are *always* in a hurry.

Particularly when it comes to evangelism.

For some reason when I was growing up, I felt this urgency related to evangelism more than anything else. Many motivational sermons, designed to get people in the pews busy, have a common theme: "We must act now!" We are passionately called to respond and take action as quickly as possible.

Many of us have been encouraged to learn all that we can so we can meticulously navigate through any situation and save the lost. And that's not necessarily a bad thing.

Sometimes we do need to move in the "now."

But for the most part, I believe that is the exception to the rule.

Here's why: Thinking that way puts pressure on the carrier of the good news that God never intended.

Sharing the good news should just flow from the inside—an overflow—a leak.

I have heard—and yes, even preached—those sermons saying that we must get to work and stay busy. Those sermons are based on Jesus' words in John 9:4, *"We must work the works of Him who sent Me as long as it is day; night is coming when no one can work."*

I thought Jesus was saying we must spread the gospel with urgency because, at some point in the future, we would no longer be able to.

But…that is not what this Scripture means.

This verse actually refers to the Church coming together as one bride and getting herself ready for the bridegroom—Jesus. It is talking about moving together in unity, power, and purpose. The blood of Jesus will be there to save and set people free until the very end of time.

Another one of "those" sermons—which I have had the honor of both listening to and preaching—is related to the 10/40 window. Roughly two-thirds of the world's population lives within a region in the eastern hemisphere located between 10 and 40 degrees north of the equator and composed of countries that, for the most part, have little exposure to the gospel or are hostile toward it. Typically, this sermon ends with an appeal to the tune of, "We need to move now while the window is open!"

It might seem like a great motivation from the pulpit, but in the pews, it feels like a guilt trip.

Fortunately, I eventually realized that Jesus doesn't need an open window or an open door.

He walks through walls!

Okay, I don't want you to get your dander up. Sermons like this do serve a purpose. My point is not to make light of the above examples. It may seem like I'm taking the need for evangelism lightly, but in reality, I'm building a case for each person's soul.

Don't pre-judge. Just keep reading.

It Doesn't Depend on Me

I've put Jesus in a nice little box many a time in my evangelistic history. I didn't do it to justify something I wasn't keen about. I simply did it because of my personal drive—and my personal limitations. I did know that God the Father absolutely loves people. That is why He gave His only Son for them.

What I didn't understand is that He loves them so much that He isn't about to let their salvation depend totally on one person.

And because I wasn't aware of this yet, I lived with this inner sense of urgency all rooted in a wrong belief about how much depended on me.

I was motivated by thoughts like, "If I don't witness to this person, he will never get saved, and his blood will be on my head."

It was like living constantly on code red emergency— every time I passed someone who wasn't a Christian. It was stressful.

Many Christians, like me, have spent years living under pressure to perform or guilt because they lack a good performance record.

Not only does thinking like that kill all of our joy in evangelism, but it is also a wrong understanding of God's heart. First Timothy 2:3-4 says, *"This is good and acceptable in the sight of God our Savior, who desires all men to be saved and to come to the knowledge of the truth."* This verse is very important. It tells us that God desires that all people would come to know His Son as Lord and Savior.

God is the one who gave all so that all may come to Him.

He's the great initiator, and He cares about the souls of people much more than we ever will or could.

I bet you've heard the phrase, "If you were the only person on this planet, God the Father still would have given His Son Jesus for you and you alone." It's a profound—and totally true—statement. And when we begin to understand it, we begin to understand His extreme love for every single person.

Okay, so here's the point. When we operate in urgency, we operate out of the assumption that we care more about people getting saved then God does.

When we strive to bring in the lost, rather than listening for Father's strategy, we betray our belief that we know how to win people's hearts better than He does.

The truth is, God loves people more than we do. He knows the key to every person's heart, and He knows the perfect timing of when to use that key. His goal is His children's hearts.

Father is exceedingly patient; He doesn't drag His children home with force, but woos them as His beloved. He pursues them in ways that prioritize relationship—not the sinner's prayer.

Ouch.

That hurts a little, doesn't it?

I used to approach people who need Jesus with this plan: Give them the gospel story, tell them anything else I heard Father saying, and then have them ask Jesus into their hearts as Lord and Savior right away.

The sinner's prayer was my goal, and I was satisfied with nothing less.

Thankfully, my ideals have shifted. Now I approach people with the understanding that God loves them so much that He will orchestrate many divine encounters in their lives—many tastes of Jesus—with the hope that, at some point along the course of their lives, they will make the decision to follow Him.

It is my privilege to be one of the divine contacts—one of the tastes of Jesus—in that person's life.

This gives me the freedom to be who God has called me to be without feeling the false pressure to "close the deal" *immediately*.

Rather than seeing myself as the only opportunity that a person might have to accept Jesus, I realize that I am just one divine encounter on a person's timeline. I know that God has orchestrated others before me and after me because of His great love for that person.

THE EXCEPTION

The rule is that God is not in a hurry and that He loves people way too much to let them to go to Hell without giving them many tastes of His love. He is continually setting up roadblocks to keep people from going there. But of course, as with almost everything, there are exceptions to the rule.

The exception is best described by the following story.

Once, I received a call from a lady in my church. Her neighbor was dying and didn't know Jesus. She asked me if I could come and talk to him about the Lord. I was on my way out of town and had to catch a flight, so I told her that I only had about fifteen minutes. She was fine with that and asked me to still come.

On the way over to his house, I talked with the Holy Spirit and said, "I know You know the situation here. Please give me the key for this man's heart."

As I entered the house, I quickly learned that he was a retired admiral in the Navy—a war hero and a highly decorated officer. It was an honor for me to speak with a man like him. As I sat and listened to him—trying not to be in a hurry, yet aware that I had to catch a flight—the Holy Spirit dropped a key into my spirit.

I asked, "Did you enjoy being in the Navy?"

"Oh, yes!" he said.

I asked him several other questions about his profession and life, and then I asked him, "Did everyone on your ship know who you were?"

"Of course they did!" he said, almost offended by the question.

"Okay, so did you know everybody on your ship?" I asked.

"No," he said.

"So you mean to tell me that everyone knew who you were and recognized their commander's voice," I asked, "And when you gave a command, whether in person or via intercom, they obeyed without hesitation, right?"

"Right," he said.

"So the men on your ship knew who you were, but had no other reason to trust you other than that they knew you were the commander of that vessel, right?"

"Right!" he said again.

I continued, "Do you think your men had to have faith in you to carry out your orders?"

He paused for a moment. Then he said, "Yes, they would have to have faith."

I looked at him and said, "I know that you have never seen God or heard His voice, but I'm asking you to have faith right now, like your men had to have in you while on your ship. Would you get on your knees with me and, by faith, ask Jesus to come in and be your Lord and Savior?"

If I had thought about what I had just asked him, I probably would have checked myself. But God had something in mind. The Holy Spirit prompted me to have him kneel, in spite of his now frail small body, because he was a proud man, and rightfully so. He slowly knelt down with me, and right there in his house, he took a step of faith and asked Jesus into his heart as Lord and Savior. Father knew what it took for this man of honor to come to Him.

I had never asked anyone to kneel before that time nor since that day.

Now, it doesn't always happen this way. Most of the time our job is to give people an encounter with Jesus. We get to partner with Father and with the rest of His kids to give people a taste of Heaven, and as they taste His love, they will never be the same. Eventually, they will reach a moment on their timelines when they are ready to make a choice for Jesus.

Though only one person or a handful of people get to participate in someone's moment of salvation, the reality is that many people along the way—living tastes of Heaven—also participated in that great reunion between Father and one of His kids.

A TASTE

Once, while I was in the checkout line at a grocery store paying for my groceries, I noticed that the man behind me was not doing so well.

I heard Father say, "You can buy his groceries if you want." He didn't say it manipulatively; He really was giving me the choice to buy them or not. I felt zero pressure.

I looked at the clerk and told her, "I would like to buy that man's groceries, too."

She looked at me sort of funny and said, "Are you sure?"

"Yes, please," I said.

The man behind me chimed in. "You don't have to do that."

I smiled and reassured him, "It would be my privilege to."

After I had paid, the man grabbed his bag and said, "Thank you so much."

"You're welcome," I said. As he walked by, I touched his shoulder. "Have a great day." I said.

And that was the end of it. I didn't add, "God Bless you," or, "Jesus loves you."

I simply said, "You're welcome," and, "Have a great day."

So many of us think we are supposed to mention Jesus in some way when we do something good for someone. But He is much bigger than we give Him credit for. Some people might ask, "What does it hurt to say, 'God bless you,' or, 'Jesus loves you.' Aren't those good ideas?"

Well, here's the thing. A good idea is only a great idea when the breath of the Holy Spirit is on it and it is carried out in His timing.

If the Spirit's not there, good ideas end up being very stressful—because we are the ones carrying the plans rather than God.

Conversely, a God idea—in His timing—is a great idea. When we partner with God's ideas, He releases supernatural favor and opens doors before us so that the whole thing seems effortless.

With a good idea, we work from our own human strength, but with a God idea, we work from His rest.

It is always better to work out of rest. Always.

What does it help or accomplish to follow through on a good idea—like adding a "Jesus loves you" to the grocery store story above? Here's why: I've seen good ideas backfire and do more damage than good.

But a God idea *never* backfires.

The God idea was to buy the man groceries.

The good idea would have been me wanting the man to know, "I'm a Christian, and that is why I am doing this."

God will get the credit, regardless of the package. In fact, often such acts of love have a lot more impact when we don't present it with a Christian veneer.

As I mentioned before, when the man walked past me, I gently put my hand on his shoulder and told him to have a great day. What I didn't tell him was in that simple and unpretentious act, I was releasing the Kingdom of Heaven to him. When I touched him as he walked by, I gave him an encounter with Jesus. He didn't realize it, but that won't minimize the effect it will have on his life.

God likes going stealth sometimes. Jesus talked about this when He told the Pharisees:

> *The kingdom of God does not come with observation; nor will they say, "See here!" or "See there!" For indeed, the kingdom of God is within you.* (Luke 17:20-21)

We affect them by virtue of our presence and the presence of the Spirit within us, not because of our spiritual namedropping. The Kingdom of Heaven is within us—whether we tell people about it or not. As a result, we impact the people we encounter—wherever we go and whatever we do.

GUILT FREE

Many Christians have felt deep guilt for years because they haven't shared Jesus like they have been instructed to. They catch a ride on a bus or a plane, the perfect place to witness, but get off without taking advantage of the opportunity. Then they feel guilty about all the people who may be going to Hell because they couldn't work up the courage to give a gospel presentation on the subway. Maybe they even saw a person who looked very sad, and they knew that the answer for that person is Jesus, but they just couldn't bring themselves to open up a conversation. Then they go home haunted by that person's face and thoughts like, "I bet that woman is going to go home and commit suicide because I didn't tell her about Jesus."

We have been indoctrinated to think that we need to bring people to the cross and lead them to repentance. And the result is that we miss many opportunities to be "tastes of Jesus" along the way. When we understand this, we will be able to walk in freedom and simply be ourselves.

When seeing a person who is broken, our natural reaction varies from giving that person a comforting smile to saying a silent prayer. More than likely, that is *exactly* what Father is doing in that moment.

He isn't preaching to them about repentance.

He is comforting them with His love.

Our job is to be Daddy's love in the moment. More often than not, that does not look like giving a gospel presentation or leading a person in the sinner's prayer.

This is not ignoring the person's need for salvation. It's loving without an agenda.

A true taste of God's love—a divine appointment in that person's timeline—will give that person one more reason to seek after Jesus.

How many times have we felt guilty because we were afraid to share the gospel and ended up doing nothing instead of capitalizing on the moment and doing what comes naturally?

How many times have we responded to a person in need like we felt we should, but then let the enemy beat us up because we didn't "close the deal"?

Too many times, that's how many.

It is time to remember the truth. God is not in a hurry.

You can't hurry love.

When we accept Jesus as our savior, we discover that God loves us too much to leave us the way we are. The Bible says that God is continually perfecting a good work in us (Phil. 1:6). The other half of that truth—for those who are yet to inherit salvation—is that He loves them too much to leave their eternal destiny up to chance or to just one person.

Don't worry about "closing the deal" or needing to drop hints so that people know you are a Christian or that Jesus loves them.

As you go about your business today, look for opportunities to simply "be" love to people. Be free to be yourself, listen to the Holy Spirit, then watch and be amazed by what God will do through you. It will be extraordinary. And extraordinary is what happens when you take the red pill.

Don't know what the red pill is? That's okay—it's what the next chapter is all about.

THE RED PILL

I vividly remember watching the movie *The Matrix* for the first time. My buddy Mark and I walked out of the theater after the movie, amazed by what we just witnessed. It was unlike any other movie we had ever seen—from the cinematography, to the message, to the acting.

We loved it.

There was a particular scene that stood out to both of us—the scene where Neo takes the red pill.

In this scene, the two main characters, Morpheus—the one who has seen the truth—and Neo—the one who seeks the truth—meet. Neo has spent his entire life searching for the truth. He could never accept the status quo, and as a result, he found himself in a precarious situation.

Then Neo meets Morpheus, who asks him a simple but life-altering question that involves making a choice between a red pill and a blue one.

If Neo chooses the blue pill, his life will continue as is, blissfully blind to reality.

However, if he chooses the red pill, he will not be able to turn back from the truth. He will discover the answers that he has been looking for and will experience just how far down the rabbit hole goes. Neo chooses the red pill, and so begins his journey into the unknown.

We all face a similar choice in our relationship with God.

Will we "take the red pill" and invite His plans into our lives—without any escape clause?

Will we give Him full reign over our futures, full permission to prune our lives according to His design?

Or would we rather take the blue pill of comfortable "life as usual"?

The choice to give our lives to the Lord is a red pill choice. But after we are believers, we continue to choose the red pill over and over by living a life of surrender. We do it by inviting God into every aspect of our lives and by praying "stupid" prayers like "Lord, break me!"

From the outside, one could look at prayers, like the "Lord, break me!" prayer, and wonder, *What in the world was he thinking?* Well, I personally wasn't thinking when I prayed that one. I wasn't evaluating the outcome or even the promise of Scripture that God is faithful to answer (1 Cor. 1:9).

Sure enough, God did answer my prayer.

He broke me, and it wasn't pleasant. In fact, it hurt quite a bit.

However, I still ask the Lord to keep me broken because He can only use a broken and contrite heart.

Okay. There is no such thing as a "stupid" prayer. Prayer is simply communication with God, and He always loves it when we talk with Him. But I think the term *stupid* fits pretty well in this analogy because it expresses the high risk those prayers entail.

To an onlooker, Neo's choice of the red pill may seem pretty foolish. He had no idea what would happen to him on the other side or even if he would survive. But Neo was driven by a desire for truth, and that desire caused him to risk *everything* in his search for answers.

Another one of my favorite "stupid" prayers is, "Lord, give me patience." The results of that prayer are easy to imagine—people and situations that try my patience. Often, when we pray "stupid prayers," we pray with our whole hearts, without considering what that prayer will cost us. When we realize the risk we're taking and the price of our prayers—and we choose them anyway—we become like Neo. Our value for truth causes us to step out in faith and pray the red pill prayers.

I have prayed many "stupid" prayers, and I suppose I will continue to pray them for as long as I live. These are those prayers where I throw myself into God's hands saying, "Do with me what You will!" There is nothing even remotely safe about that prayer.

I pray those prayers because I'm not driven by my need for safety or comfort.

I pray them because I am driven by my need for intimacy with God.

More than once, I have looked back at a "stupid" prayer and thought, *I wish I had known what I was getting myself into.*

Nevertheless, the cost of my prayers will not deter me from praying them. It may cause me to think twice about it beforehand, but in the end, I pray them anyway because I am compelled by my love for Father and a longing for His truth.

Most likely, in your lifetime, you have prayed something to the effect of, "I will do anything You want me to do, Father." You may have even followed it up with other statements of absolute surrender, like, "Father, I give You permission to use me however You want, no strings attached." When you prayed, you may not have considered the risk involved.

That is your red pill. Now you know the risk you're taking.

The question is, with eyes wide open: Are you ready to go all the way with God? Are you ready to take the red pill?

In fact, why don't we do it right now? Pray with me again: "Father, take all of me, and do whatever You want with me. I am Yours."

Feels good, and kind of scary, doesn't it?

It's like setting off on a grand adventure into the unknown. It is also exactly where God wants you to be.

Once you have taken the red pill, the sky is the limit.

CALLED

I have a very good friend who has an unusual but fascinating ministry.

In fact, I have never seen or heard of another ministry that does what his does.

Sometimes it seems like he is ahead of his time, especially because of the "deer-in-headlights" looks he gets from others when he describes his ministry. Notwithstanding the stares or the unconventional nature of what they do, this man and his wife have no doubt that God has given them this particular call.

Without going into great detail of the ins and outs of what he does, the point is that he has been *called*.

As a husband and father, my friend has a responsibility to provide for his family. But shifting a career focus and starting a new ministry is anything but easy—a myriad of things need to happen on limited time and budget. Their journey has been anything but effortless or painless.

We know that God is good, that we are His children, and that He loves us very much. However, I also know that before we can carry what He desires us to carry, more than likely testing, testing, and more testing must take place first.

Sometimes we like to imagine that, because God loves us, everything will simply come together without any struggle or pain. My friend, probably like many who are reading this book, would love to be in full-time ministry. He has a significant call of God on his life, and his heart longs to be walking in the fullness of that call. Yet he is in the in-between time—the time between when he said *yes* to the call and when he will finally be walking in the fullness of his dream.

Recently, I received a phone call from him.

He was not very happy.

In fact, he was pretty down.

He had to, in his mind, lay down the call on his life and find employment to feed his family. He saw this as a spiritual demotion. If that wasn't enough, some of his friends and family had begun to look down on him because they thought he wasn't being responsible in the first place and never should have ventured into ministry. Like the friends of Job, people were quick to give their opinions.

The problem was that these people—who were so quick to criticize—had not taken the red pill.

They had not given God an unqualified, unreasonable, and risky yes to whatever He might say.

This friend had, and his decisions stemmed from his experience with Father.

After I talked with him, I got off the phone and began to pray. During that time, Father gave me a great word. So I called him back and asked him a few questions. First I asked, "Do you believe that God wants the best for you?"

"Yes." he said.

"Do you believe that God is good?" I asked.

Again, he responded, "Yes, I do."

Finally, I asked, "Do you know beyond a shadow of doubt that you have been called to do this ministry?"

"Yep. Beyond a shadow of a doubt," he said.

I then reminded him of the time he had taken the red pill.

"You gave God permission to use you to do whatever He wants, right?" I asked.

"Yes, I did." he responded quietly. He knew what was coming.

I took a breath and went on, "Do you believe that God loves the lost so much that He would alter one believer's life just so they could get a taste of Jesus and never be the same?"

"Yes!"

"You prayed a prayer that gave Father permission to have His way with you," I continued. "He took you at face value and said to His angels, 'Hey, we can use this guy!' Heaven shouted! Then they got busy seeing who needed an encounter with Jesus."

He was quiet, but I could feel him processing. I went on, "Is it possible that Father loves those who haven't accepted His Son as Lord and Savior so much that He would interrupt your life, ministry, and call because you gave Him permission to—just to save one?"

There was a new sense of freedom in his voice when he answered.

"Absolutely, yes."

And with those words, a shift happened in his heart. His entire outlook instantly changed. No longer did he dread going to work; instead, he was ecstatic. He saw that Father loves him so much that He's taking him along the best path—the path that makes dreams become reality.

God...Shocked?

Many times our actions show that we think God is shocked by our circumstances.

Can you imagine God looking puzzled and saying to the angels, "Wow, I didn't see that one coming! Did you?"

As funny as that sounds, our whining or our lack of faith shows that, subconsciously, we believe that very scenario. The truth is, Father has not only *our* best in mind, but also the best of those who are on the journey toward being saved. Our goal then, is no longer the dream, but the journey.

Why?

Because it's on the journey that our dreams come true.

Okay, I'm going to be honest, as if I haven't been throughout this book. My gut response to the popular saying, "The joy is in the journey," usually goes something like, "Yeah right! Don't you know that I have things to do and people to see? And don't you know that sometimes the journey is highly overrated?"

I've always considered myself a goal-oriented person who can accomplish anything I set my mind to. Sometimes I write out a list just so I can cross stuff off as I go about the day.

Let's just say I'm driven.

And the problem with being driven and goal-oriented is that I easily miss the beauty of simply moving forward.

During our Friday Night Strikes in San Francisco, we would encounter the streets with the love of God through an army of people, often times from different churches and ministries.

We divided into teams and divvied up the food, socks, blankets, and other items that we were giving out that night. Then we sent the teams out to their assigned streets. We started at the United Nations plaza downtown and, depending on the number of people we had on a particular night, tried to cover as much of the Tenderloin as possible.

After several years of these outreaches, the homeless knew we would be there every Friday, and they often would intercept the teams on their way to their assigned locations.

I could always tell when team leaders were goal-oriented because they would not give anything out to the homeless people who approached them.

Instead, they would tell them that their supplies were intended for another area.

Ironic, isn't it?

The whole purpose of being on the streets was to give people a taste of Jesus, no matter where they were. Many of the goal-oriented people, however, were focused on getting to their assigned areas, and they needed to be in that location before beginning to minister the love of God.

It sounds silly, but it actually happens a lot.

Chances are, you have many things that you need to do today. Make a list in your mind or on a piece of paper of all those little things that have to get done. Now think about the things you did yesterday. Did you accomplish everything you had on your list?

Prepare yourself for a reality check: It is not important whether you completed your list or not.

What's important is if you took advantage of the journey.

The Divine Set-Up

If you have taken the red pill, then you can rest assured that God has set up many divine encounters for you *every* day. In my life, I have often chosen to ignore these divine set-ups, or I have missed the opportunities God offered to me.

I want to open your eyes so that you become more aware of the things going on around you. Not one of the "distractions" you encounter takes God by surprise, and you must consider whether He has placed them in your path for a reason.

In other words, you have a divinely given opportunity to give people a taste of Jesus everyday, everywhere.

God is good, and your steps are ordered by Him.

Ask Him to help you not only enjoy the journey, but also be acutely aware of the faces around you who need Jesus. As you pray that, I promise your awareness will broaden and joy will fill your heart.

This walk with Jesus is an E-ticket ride. When you used to visit Disneyland, you would need a ticket to get on the rides. Different tickets gave you access to different levels of rides, and you needed the E-ticket if you wanted to ride all of the best rides.

Being a Christian isn't supposed to be like riding the Ferris Wheel.

It's much more like strapping into the "biggest and baddest" roller coaster you can imagine.

Praying the risky prayers and walking with Jesus is not safe or comfortable. When Neo took the red pill, he stepped into a world of danger. The comfortable life disappeared. But in its place, he found truth, adventure, purpose, and love.

In the C. S. Lewis classic, *The Lion, the Witch, and the Wardrobe*, Aslan the lion, who is a type of Christ, is described this way: "He's not safe, but he's good." That's the assurance we have.

Giving Jesus full control of our lives isn't necessarily safe.

It is a big risk.

But it is also a calculated risk, based on the fact that God is, in fact, very good.

TROPHIES

Once you've given Jesus full control, you can expect to get some pretty awesome testimonies. But let me give you a little tip. Don't collect trophies.

Keep your focus where it should be.

Jesus.

A prophet friend of mine gave me a peculiar word several years ago, and I feel it is important not only for me, but also for all you reading this book—and I want to share it now before this last chapter ends.

My friend began the word by going into great detail about my future and what I would see in the years to come. He told me he saw me preaching before thousands upon thousands of people. He said blind eyes would be opened, deaf ears would hear, lame people would walk, diseases would leave, demon-possessed people would be delivered, thousands would come to know Jesus as Lord and Savior, and dead people would be brought to the meetings and go home alive and well.

What a word!

I was excited and humbled by it. My friend listed everything I have always dreamed about.

Then he continued, "When you are done with that particular meeting, I have some very important instructions for you for when you get back to your hotel room."

"Okay." I said, not having a clue where he was going with this.

"Get ready for bed, go into the bathroom, and sit by the toilet. Lift the lid and tell the toilet everything that happened that night. Don't leave anything out; tell of all of the healings, deliverances, salvations, and dead being raised. Exhaust your memory of everything that God did that night. When you can't remember anything else, close the lid of the toilet, flush it, wash your hands, and go to bed. As you lay there in bed, look to Father in Heaven and say, 'Thanks, Dad! That was fun. What do You want to do tomorrow? You want me to take the kids fishing? Okay, I'll see you in the morning.'"

He continued, "You are going to experience wonderful things in this life. Your deepest desires will come to pass, but you must remember this simple story. You are blessed to participate with the Father in setting the captives free and destroying the works of the enemy, but that is not your focus. When all is said and done, get back to the main thing, which is your relationship with Father."

This word changed my life. It's a constant reminder that I am co-laboring with my Father. I am not alone in making plans, but am joining with His.

That is why I ask, "What do you want to do tomorrow? Go fishing?" I am a self-starter, a type-A personality, and sometimes this is hard for me to do.

Driven people like to complete tasks.

We like to decide what we're going to do and then do it.

However, when we partner with Father, healing the masses and seeing the lost come to know Jesus as Lord and Savior is *just* as significant to Him as taking my kids fishing the following day.

It's about doing what He's doing, and whatever that is, that's what we need to be doing to.

Nevertheless, it is very easy to collect spiritual trophies.

Dragon Slayer

I prayed once for a lady who had a Komodo dragon on her chest—not literally, but spiritually. I had previously had a dream about how I should take this dragon off of her and that she would be healed when I did. When I woke up, I remembered the dream, and I figured it was too bizarre to be a "pizza dream." I reluctantly obeyed the Lord by praying for this woman and pulling the dragon off her chest, just as I had seen in the dream. When I did, she was instantly set free from the demonic spirit and healed from a disease that she had suffered with for over twenty years.

Now here is the point: If I started referring to myself as a "dragon slayer" and went around looking for spiritual dragons to confront—unless that was something God had specifically told me to do—I would be collecting a spiritual trophy. I would be finding identity in what I had accomplished rather than in my relationship as a son to my Father.

And because my identity had become about my success, I would continue to do what I had been successful in, even if Father was trying to lead me somewhere else.

This example may sound silly, but the reality is that many times we learn something from God, and then we rely on the thing we learned instead of the One who taught us.

Personally, I hope I never see another one of those dragons.

Collecting trophies takes us away from Father and gradually leads us into independence and self-sufficiency. Eventually, we find ourselves far from His heart because we forgot to treasure the main thing.

We found a way to get results quickly, but exacted a price in our relationship with Father.

If we get a lot done that He didn't ask us to do, it doesn't mean much. This is the sobering reality painted in Corinthians:

> *For no other foundation can anyone lay than that which is laid, which is Jesus Christ. Now if anyone builds on this foundation with gold, silver, precious stones, wood, hay, straw, each one's work will become clear; for the Day will declare it, because it will be revealed by fire; and the fire will test each one's work, of what sort it is. If anyone's work which he has built on it endures, he will receive a reward. If anyone's work is burned, he will suffer loss; but he himself will be saved, yet so as through fire.* (1 Cor. 3:11-15)

Please don't miss this. Tools, methods, effective strategies, and prayers (to name a few things) are good and wonderful—unless they become more than mere tools that the Holy Spirit can use through us. If we begin to rely on them *instead* of Father, we are in trouble.

That is the main message of the prophetic word I received, and it is the main thing that I want you to remember.

Keep the main thing the main thing—and Father must be the main thing.

What He is doing, and where His anointing is, is all that matters. And when we understand that, our job becomes very simple. All we have to do is follow.

ALL FOR LOVE

We have officially reached the end of this book. And before you shut the cover and put it back on the shelf, or pass it along to someone else, I want to leave you with some advice.

It's this: Follow Father, and move where He moves.

If you take anything away from these pages, I hope and pray it's that.

The Holy Spirit will quicken our spirits when He wants us to participate in what He's doing. Sometimes Father will remind us of something that we did that worked before, and when He does this, we should do it again.

It gets dangerous when we are not listening to God, only remember what worked last time, and try to do the same thing again without any Holy Spirit nudging. I am not referring to the principle spelled out in Revelation 19:10, *"…the testimony of Jesus is the spirit of prophecy."* That's when we hear of a testimony of what Jesus has done and it becomes a prophetic word that we, as the hearers, can receive for our own lives. Remember when Mark grabbed a man's broken foot and commanded it to be healed—simply because we had just heard a testimony of someone doing this very thing? That was pulling on the testimony of a miracle and asking God to do it again in our lives.

It was not rote repetition.

When we pulled on that testimony, God released a similar miracle for the man we encountered.

Now, we do not do this every time we encounter a man with a broken foot. That would be creating a method and collecting a trophy. We would be doing something over and over again, not because the Holy Spirit told us to, but because it worked the first time we tried it.

Are you getting it? Our purpose in life is this: to get as close to Father's heart as we can and to follow His lead—to do what He's doing and say what He's saying.

Anything else is a monument that will not count for much.

This is why, when all is said and done, we must say, "Thank You, Father, for allowing me to partner with You today. What do You want to do tomorrow? Goodnight, Dad!" And we must say it because we know that love is the key.

When we pray for the sick, love must be the motivation.

When we prophesy, love has to be at the center.

When we feed the hungry, it must be for love.

Love must be the reason for all that we do.

Keep it simple.

Listen to the Holy Spirit inside.

He always knows what is best.

Remember: The bottom line is not the sinner's prayer, but giving people a taste of Jesus, an experience from Heaven.

God is not in a hurry, and He loves people way too much to casually let them die. He will exhaust Heaven to give them a taste of His Son and the joy of redemption.

You have more power than you know by just leaking Jesus onto people through a word, a smile, or a helping hand.

He will give you keys to people's hearts as you love Him and choose to love them.

Enjoy God, enjoy His creation, and enjoy people.

After all, you are His beloved!

And that's what being Jesus to the world looks like.

Now get out there and start loving.

Because it really is that simple.

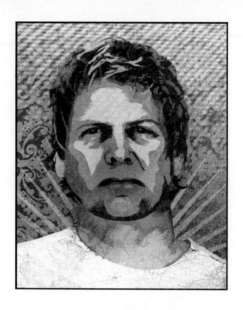

BIOGRAPHY

Bob Johnson is a radical lover to the lost and the broken. He has a passion for treating "Hell's Trash" like "Heaven's Treasures." His innovative approach to loving people has stirred many to do *whatever it takes* to bring the lost into the Kingdom of God.

Bob is a fifth-generation preacher with a total of nine generations of preachers on his dad and mom's sides combined. He is married to his soul mate, Kimberly, and combined, they have six children (so far) with more to come! Bob and Kimberly ministered in the city of San Francisco for many years. It is there that they defined their life message. They became faith with "skin on" as they loved the homeless, the prostitutes, street people and inner-city kids. They continue to live out that life message today through the vision of being, "Jesus to the World."

Bob and Kimberly currently live in Redding, California, and passionately pursue the Father's heart in many ways, from heavy social injustice issues like child trafficking to practical adventures like water purification.

ENDNOTES

CHAPTER 6

1. A prophetic word is a like a word of encouragement, but it is also more than that. God gives you a glimpse of the treasures inside someone and you point them out, breathing hope and life deep inside of the person you are speaking to.

CHAPTER 8

1. THE MATRIX
(Sydney, Australia: Warner Bros. Pictures, 1999).

2. THE LION, THE WITCH, AND THE WARDROBE
© C.S. Lewis Pte Ltd., 1950.

red arrow

Red Arrow Media is a company of media professionals with diverse, cosmopolitan backgrounds and a wealth of experience, all united by our desire to create, produce, and distribute excellent literary texts and other media worldwide. We offer a comprehensive menu of publishing services and specialize in helping both budding and seasoned authors find their literary voice, write and edit their texts, and create powerful and pleasing interior and exterior designs. We also connect our authors with a plethora of other media services, from printing and distribution to bookselling, website development, publicity campaigns, photography, and video production.

www.redarrowmedia.com

$19.97

ISBN 978-0-9884992-1-8

51997>

9 780988 499218